'IT'S NOT JUST ABOUT BLACK AND WHITE, MISS'

'IT'S NOT JUST ABOUT BLACK AND WHITE, MISS'

Sally Elton-Chalcraft

Trentham Books

Stoke on Trent, UK and Sterling, USA

Trentham Books Limited
Westview House   22883 Quicksilver Drive
734 London Road   Sterling
Oakhill   VA 20166-2012
Stoke on Trent   USA
Staffordshire
England ST4 5NP

First published 2009

British Library Cataloguing-in-Publication Data
A catalogue record for this book is available from the British Library

ISBN: 978 1 85856 437 1

Cover photograph: Sally Elton-Chalcraft

Designed and typeset by Trentham Books Ltd, Chester and printed
in Great Britain by Henry Ling Ltd, Dorchester.

Contents

Acknowledgments

I would like to thank everyone who was involved in supporting the completion of the piece of research from which this book sprang – the staff and children at all the schools who participated in the research, my PhD supervisors Professor Marie Parker-Jenkins, Professor John Hinnells and Dr Brian Hall and my examiners Professor Paul Weller and Professor Robert Jackson. Thanks also to the University of Derby for awarding me the Millennium bursary to undertake the research. Numerous colleagues and students from both the University of Derby and my present institution, the University of Cumbria, (formerly St Martin's College) have helped, in a variety of ways, to keep me on task – for which I am most grateful – particular thanks to Carrie Mercier who has given me time and space, Diane Warner, Dr John Hammond and students who made comments on drafts and Maria Chippendale who has kept me company during holiday times while working on the book! Particular thanks to Gillian Klein and all at Trentham Books.

To my family and friends I owe a deep gratitude for their support- especially to my late mother, Margaret Elton who would have been so proud to know I wrote a book, and to my brother Robert Elton who helped proof read the initial research. My late father, Granger, and my late sister, Rosemary, died before I began the book but I would like to acknowledge their encouragement in former years which gave me the confidence to engage in this research.

My husband, Professor David Chalcraft, has been incredibly supportive, and encouraging from start to finish – reading drafts, proof reading and engaging in conversations – often amidst the chatter, banging and singing of our three beautiful children, Holly, Jetta and Izaak. My children have been very patient sharing me with each other, and the research. Thank you.

Foreword

Paul Weller

D r. Elton-Chalcraft sets out an important agenda and set of considerations for education professionals, policy-makers and parents. The book is not, as it might have been, merely a set of interesting academic opinions, or even only the sharing of professional teaching experience. Rather, it is rooted in rigorous research that draws upon, and makes accessible to a wider public, her doctoral research project at the University of Derby, conducted alongside her professional practice as a school teacher and her work in the training of teachers at the Universities of both Derby and Cumbria.

The book records and disseminates important findings about how a sample of children in four English primary schools of varied ethnic mixes view questions of identity in relation to 'race' and 'ethnicity'; and about how these questions touch upon matters of 'religion' and culture' – all of which are, of course, contested terms in relation to the phenomena to which they are intended to point. But however these concepts are understood, the plurality of ethnicity, religion, belief and culture that characterises classrooms of today is affirmed as being a critically important dimension of what must be taken seriously and wrestled with by educators and other stakeholders in our multicultural society.

What is particularly challenging and distinctive about what the author has attempted to do in this book is the way in which she underlines the importance that adults take on board – as far as is possible – a child-centred perspective on matters that are generally debated by adults and then decided by adults alone.

While adopting a child's perspective is something that one wonders whether an adult can ever fully attain, the methodological effort to do so that permeates this book is surely worth making. In this attempt, Dr. Elton-Chalcraft seems somehow to have managed to achieve a rare integration of her training as a teacher; her work as a trainer of teachers; her odyssey as a researcher; and last but perhaps not least, her experience and orientation as a parent.

Such integration seems to me to shine through the overall approach that the author both adopts herself and encourages others to adopt. The children she writes about are truly seen as people in their own right and not reduced to the mere provisional status of 'adults in the making'.

Paul Weller, Professor of Inter-Religious Relations and Head of Research and Commercial Development, Faculty of Education, Health & Sciences, University of Derby

1
Introduction

I think we should have like more black people ... more white people in black areas and more black people in white areas ... then we'll get to know what they are like and it'll stop most wars. (Cassie, a white girl from a mainly white school)

Are children in some types of schools more racist than others?
Are some children born racist and others naturally antiracist?
Are children less racist than adults?
What do children think about their own and other cultures?

These were the questions that drove my research with 9 and 10 year old children in a variety of schools in central England. I spent the best part of a year listening to what year 5 children in city, town and village schools chose to tell me about their lives, racism and their attitudes towards different cultures. This book reports on what I discovered about children's perceptions of their own and other cultures, and the opportunities or lack of them presented to them in school to explore issues of diversity. It goes some way to identifying a connection between what children know about diversity and their attitudes towards it.

This chapter looks at

- the educational backdrop to the research, the content-driven curriculum

- issues surrounding research concerning children's attitudes to race

- the concept of racism

1

■ key racist incidents that have affected policy and practice

■ the evolution of education and race

As teachers we may be unaware of the racism which exists in our school community until something happens which forces it to the surface.

It is against the law to discriminate against someone because of their ethnicity, and racial incidents in schools are supposed to be monitored. All children should be enabled to reach their potential irrespective of their social or ethnic background (DfES, 2006; Parker-Jenkins *et al*, 2007). The concept of social cohesion has become an important value in education and many books offer guidance to support schools in tackling racism and promoting inclusive education and social cohesion (for example Dadzie, 2000; Knowles and Ridley, 2005; Parker-Jenkins *et al*, 2007). It is within this context that the research took place and the book explores the links between the curriculum and the child's own multicultural awareness.

Cassie and Saz, both white children from Exforth, a predominantly white school, discuss their own ethnicity:

Cassie: I don't know much about them [the Black relatives she had talked about earlier] – they are really distant but I know how I'm related to them

Saz: Everyone's related to everyone

Sally: Are they?

Saz: Yeah cos in a way I'm related to her – only met up with her when I got to X town

Sally: How do you know you are related to each other?

Saz: Because of Adam and Eve the first people on the planet

Cassie: Yeah, but I believe that my great great great grandad was a gorilla or something.

Sally: Do you believe that?

Saz: No – I believe that humans were humans from the start. If we did start from gorillas then gorillas wouldn't be around now. And the gorillas in cages have been there for hundreds of years. They would have evolved by now so I don't really think about it

Sally: Have you thought that yourself or have your family told you?

Saz: I saw it on Walking with Dinosaurs – something like that and history programmes on BBC 2.

2

The children in my research told me about their attitudes towards their own and other cultures. They said that their parents, television and school had contributed to their understanding.

Educational context

Children's attitudes are to some degree a consequence of the curriculum so it is helpful to start with the educational context. This section describes my understanding of the educational scene in England where the research took place and explains why I consider the curriculum to be value-laden.

The National Curriculum in England (QCA, 1999) is concerned predominantly with 'content' which we teachers are required to impart to children (Grimmitt, 2000). Perhaps weighed down by the burden of paperwork and preparation for Ofsted visits and SATS (Standard Assessment Tests, 2006), we may not have time to consider why we are teaching what we are teaching; we may feel we have subscribed to a culture where we want to be told what the content is and be allowed to get on and teach it. But the educational climate does affect what is taught, and also why and how it is taught.

If teachers are engaged in a content-driven rather than child-centred curriculum, this will have an impact on values. The content-centred curriculum is ready made – with intrinsic but often hidden values (Grimmitt, 2000). Whereas the child-centred curriculum is more concerned with a child's involvement in their learning, and less imposition of externally determined values. Sometimes teachers, especially new teachers and student teachers, find it comforting to have the curriculum prescribed; certainly it is less challenging when teaching is reduced simply to the management of tasks which have been determined by someone else. The teacher merely has to be 'trained' to impart the curriculum in the most efficient way (Twiselton, 2004, 2006).

This book explores the links between the content-driven curriculum with its implicit values, and the child's own multicultural awareness. Children have had little influence on what and how they are taught (Devine, 2003). The *Independent Review of the Primary Curriculum* (Rose, 2008) tries to ensure that the curriculum is more child-centred, but the children in my research were at school when the content-centred National Curriculum was in force.

Teachers are beginning to question the methods of teaching and learning that have been imposed and many are themselves engaging in research to ascertain which strategies, values and methods suit their pupils' learning. Yet not all teachers think of themselves as reflective practitioners and practitioner researchers (Ollerton, 2008) because many have themselves been educated in a prescriptive system. It is those who view teacher education as education rather than training who see teaching and learning as a research-based profession.

Researching children's attitudes towards race

Some student teachers I work with do not realise that education is value-laden. They think that research can be conducted in a value-free manner. But no researcher can simply pose a research question (in my case 'what is a child's knowledge and what are their attitudes concerning their own and other cultures?') and design a study, collect data, analyse it and (like an input/output machine) produce an answer. Rather, the researcher needs to consider her position about the nature of the concepts and issues under scrutiny (in my case culture, identity and racism). Delanty and Strydom argue that 'an external reality exists which is independent of human consciousness yet can nevertheless be known' (2003:376). But constructivism argues that all science is constructed by social actors.

I subscribe to the constructivist rather than the realist approach because I believe there is no such thing as 'Asian culture', 'white culture', 'African-Caribbean culture' which exist in isolation. I was not expecting children in my study to describe an actual culture which existed out there which could be found if the researcher knew where to find it. Rather, I think that children's attitudes and knowledge refer to cultures – their own and other people's – which are socially constructed.

The children in my research understood that I wanted to find out their perceptions. As Manpreet, a British Asian Sikh girl from Rarnlow school, observed: 'So you want to find out what we think – like we're a computer with information and you click on it.'

Similarly Mehvesh, a British Asian Muslim girl from one of the pilot multi-ethnic schools, said: 'We are like dictionaries Miss, you can look things up in us.' My research methods are described in detail in the appendix.

4

I also assume that a child's perception might differ from an adult's (Alderson, 2000), and I was interested in exploring the different kinds of constructions the children described to me. Interestingly, the children themselves initially spoke in realist language about these cultures. Bart, a white boy from Bently school said:

> Bart: There are only two Hindus that I know – Bin Laden and Daljit, but I'm not sure about Daljit.
>
> Sally: So you think Bin Laden is Hindu?
>
> Bart: Yeah cos he wears that turban.

Bart talked in negative terms about Hindus as well as getting it wrong by thinking that Bin Laden, a Muslim, and Daljit, a Sikh, were Hindus. Bart was referring to his own socially constructed version of a Hindu – ie. a leader of a terrorist organisation as socially constructed by the media.

I adopted a post-modern feminist perspective in both the research and my interpretation of the data and tried to be transparent about who I am and why I chose to undertake the research – namely to encourage inter-cultural relations, and particularly to work towards the abolition of racist, sexist, adultist and classist attitudes in schools. But I did not challenge racist comments at any interview, so allowing children to articulate views such as those below. Kurt from Bently school discussed his thoughts about people from a different culture. Kurt is of dual heritage, a Jamaican mother and white father. Jamie is white.

> Kurt: They're ugly [giggles]
>
> Sally: They're ugly – so you think people who aren't the same culture as you are ugly?
>
> Kurt: Yeah
>
> Sally: Why do you say that?
>
> Kurt: because they've got funny eyes and different to ours, ours are like
>
> that, their's are bozeyed [making facial gestures].
>
> Jamie: Yeah but Heidi [Kurt's girlfriend] is a different culture to you and everyone else in ... and some people in this thing, in this school, has different culture to you but you like 'em – you're friends with 'em. So I don't know what you're pointing that for – ugly. [pause] And so if Heidi's got a different culture to you are you gonna dump her?
>
> Kurt: [embarrassed giggle] Nnooo.

The group interview provided a forum for the children to challenge each other and thus confirm or change their opinions, as the above extract shows. At the time of the interview I tried not to impose any values, but later at the presentation of my preliminary findings the children and I discussed racism and antiracism and the children encouraged each other to adopt an antiracist stance.

The social construction of culture

I found that when children discussed their views about different cultures they often drew on evidence which had been constructed by the media. Strinati, in his book *Popular culture* (1995), discusses the postmodern view of culture as a social construct. He outlines sociologies of popular culture which can be summarised as follows.

- The liberal view that mass media used to hold up a mirror to reality in which we were able to look at ourselves and reality
- The radical rejoinder that mass media distorted the image
- The view that the media played a part in constructing our sense of being a part of this reality; and
- The mirror IS the reality. (Summarised from Strinati, 1995:224)

What the children in my study told me about Muslims, for example, was what they had seen on television. One is led to believe that postmodern views of popular culture are social constructions of reality; we take the mirror image to be reality, and this is a distorted image. Futhermore, the actual part of reality chosen to be reflected in the mirror is provided by the media. Television presents a version of reality which viewers believe to be real. Strinati discusses television and consumerism as being the only sources for identity formation, but 'these are illusory' (p238). I considered the impact of television, amongst other influences, on the children's attitudes and knowledge of their own and other cultures, and how the media amplification of events influences their construction of reality.

Children's constructions of culture are also informed by the presentation of different cultures in school resources, and also what they see in the community. James, Liam and Nicola, all three British white children from Bently (a predominantly white school in a multicultural city) discuss Asian culture. They often interspersed misconceptions with accurate knowledge and for this reason I quote at length.

6

James: Asians, they eat different things and they believe in different things and most of them own shops. ... Miss there's another, they wear different clothes.

Sally: What kind of clothes do they wear then?

James: Like dresses and turbans

Sally: How do you know that?

James: By looking at pictures of them at school

Nicola: Emm most of them have shops – emm they believe they have to keep their face covered because of their religion, most of them

Sally: Right

Liam: Some eat curry and they believe in lots and lots of gods and wear turbans and shoes

James: Miss and it [a picture of a Muslim Asian heritage family in their home] shows some things what they believe in on the walls – them pictures

Nicola: Miss they're actually eating the same food that we would – they're eating some of the things that we would and some different

James: Cos like when like ... For example, Pakistani, we go to church they go to Mosque. That looks like a mosque – I've seen it on the telly

Sally: Right OK – do you think that's a mosque?

James: Miss yeah cos they have to take their shoes off don't they?

Sally: What do you know about mosques then? What religion is that what culture is that?

Nicola: Might be...Indian

Jamie: Pakistan

Sally: Indian Pakistan – What else do they believe in – Muslims?

Jamie: Rama and Sita

Nicola: I don't....

Jamie: Miss they believe in Allah

Nicola: Don't know

Gaining trust

I spent time getting to know the children and they confided in me, as the following extract from Rarnlow multi-ethnic school shows. Before each discussion I asked the children if they were willing to talk to me and for me to take notes or tape record them (see appendix). Harvir, a British Asian Sikh girl, suggests that it is preferable to remain in one's own culture and marry within it too:

> Harvir: My uncle got married to a white person, and it's not her fault, but we Sikhs say that you should get married to the same culture as you, and people who don't, they sort of – it's kind of a sin to God, sort of. You're not meant to but some people do, and that's their decision, and my uncle did and now he doesn't believe in God. Like, his dad, who's my Granddad – he still talks to him like that but he just doesn't believe in God anymore.
>
> Sally: And, do you mind me asking – you don't have to answer any question at all, what do *you* think about that?
>
> Harvir: I think well because I am a Sikh it was a wrong thing to do but because he's older than me I can't really say to him you're stupid, you're naughty – you shouldn't have done this. It's his decision if he's done that we can't change him and say divorce her or something like that. So what's done is done.
>
> Sally: And is that your opinion or is that perhaps what your parents [think]?
>
> Harvir: That's my opinion I don't know what my parents think ... Mainly what people tell you is to be, not to become, another religion just because it's better or anything, but be what you are, be your own religion and be a good Sikh or a good Muslim or be a good Hindu or Christian
>
> Sally: Which people say this?
>
> Harvir: The people at our temple, they say that every time they do that in English they say what you look like, you are still Sikh, and no matter what anybody calls you, you should be proud of what you are and what colour you are and things like that at the Gurdwara.

The chapters in this book offer insight into the attitudes and stances towards different cultures of a range of year 5 children in four different schools in the Midlands. Over a hundred children took part in the research. I talked with them during playtimes, lunchtimes and at appropriate moments during lesson time. I also interviewed over seventy children in pairs or threes to discover what they had to say about race. Racism is an emotive and complex term which I explore next.

Racism

Anything which had elements of negative perception, was stereotypical or discriminatory I labelled as racist. The word 'racism' suggests that there are such things as 'races', and, by implication, that some are better than others, and that people can be treated unfairly and/or abusively on account of their race, or in some cases on account of their religion, where religious belief is seen as an indicator of race (Weller, 2005). Legislation on racism in the workplace (Race Relations Act, 1976, Race Relations Amendment act, 2000)

> makes it unlawful to discriminate against a person, directly or indirectly on racial grounds in: employment; education; housing; and in the provision of goods, facilities and services. (Race Relations Act, 1976)

Yet the notion of 'races' is totally discredited. The notion has been described as a social construction invented by Europeans, who believed that races were different from each other in biological ways (Boxill, 2001; Solomos, 2003). The two extracts below indicate a range of perspectives on difference. Tazia, Rosie and Zena are all girls of Asian heritage from Deasham multi-ethnic school:

> Tazia: I think they [people of a different culture] should be treated the same way as others
>
> Sally: What do you think about people who are of a different culture?
>
> Rosie: they are the same they're just a different colour to us but they have a different religion and they like, they not same as you but you shouldn't treat them different – they're just persons, people, they're not like animals or something.
>
> Zena: And I would be the same way that I always am and I wouldn't make them feel low about what I said or what I did ... I think they should be treated the same way as other people.

This point is raised again by two British Asian children and one white boy from the same school:

> Amy: Miss I think all people are the same it doesn't matter what culture they are ...
>
> Gurdeep: [I think all people are] same as me. I don't think Jesus is good or bad or my God is good or bad I think they are the same Hindus are [the] same, every culture [the same]
>
> Jess: It doesn't really matter what colour you are
>
> Gurdeep: I don't think he's poor I'm rich I think we're the same
>
> Amy: I've got a friend she's half caste, she's half English half Indian, it doesn't matter we're all the same.

This contrasts with the comments of Max, a white boy attending Bently, a predominantly white school.

> Max: My dad's ermm a racist because he don't like no brown skinned people but he does like half caste cos there's a wrestler that's half caste, De Roc
>
> Sally: So how did you describe your dad, your Dad's a what?
>
> Max: Err a racist he don't like brown skinned people but he does like half caste cos he's just fine with half castes cos he used to take the rip out of half castes but I said, don't dad, because it's a bit nasty but you can take the rip out of Hindus because I don't like them – cos it's Bin Laden he's like the boss of all the Hindus [pause] that's about all I know

Research for the Home Office undertaken by Weller *et al* (2000) highlights that religion is sometimes a factor in cases of discrimination. The Racial and Religious Hatred Act (2006) makes it illegal to incite religious hatred.

Reasons for Racism

As teachers it is important for us to understand the complexity of the concept of racism and recognise and challenge all manifestations of it. The possible underlying reasons for racism must be considered. Just as there are numerous types of racism so there have been numerous explanations. Scholars have charted the nature and development of prejudice in children (Aboud, 1988; Brown, 1998, 2008).

John and David, both white boys, and Alan, a British Asian Sikh boy who chose a western pseudonym, talk about the importance of being nice and why they think some people are not. All three are from Rarnlow multi-ethnic school.

> David: I just hate people who call people racist names
>
> John: It makes the street all not nice – we want a happy world not like umm not a sad world we want everyone to be kind to everyone else, like Chinese ...we want white people to be kind to Chinese people and Chinese people to be kind to us
>
> Sally: Why do you think people are ..well we've talked about racist, why do you think people are racist?
>
> Alan: Because they don't like our skin colour.
>
> John: They look 'funny' and sometimes when they pray or something they might get laughed at – they laugh at them because ...

10

Alan: [interrupted] Yeah and white people laugh at Indian names.

Racism is explained in cognitive psychological terms by Goodman (1964). According to his theory, individuals recognise their membership of a group which is distinct from other groups.

A second explanation dwells on personality theory:

> The prejudiced person is one who grows up in a family environment where the roles are based on dominance and submission and in which discipline is harsh and geared to rigid keeping of rules requiring conformity rather than personal responsibility. The child learns to despise weakness in himself and others and develops a desire to be associated with the powerful and strong person. (Adorno *et al*, 1950)

According to this theory, a weak scapegoat to attack is needed, but this does not account for why a particular scapegoat is chosen. I discovered that cultures of dominance presented perfect conditions for racism to flourish (see chapters 5 and 8).

A third explanation, the socio conflict theory, has two elements. Firstly, prejudice arises out of rivalry between groups that are fighting for the same resources, resulting in 'out' group hostility. The second is rooted in the Marxist belief of capitalist exploitation. However as Aboud states, it is not enough to mix children up in a multi-ethnic school in the hope of eradicating prejudice and in particular racism, as proponents of the 'contact theory' suggest (Aboud, 1988:82; also this book chapter 8). There is a weakness in the social reflection theory which Aboud relates to the significance of the age of the child (1988:100). The younger child is more likely to follow parental directives whereas the older child is more likely to 'attend to the individual qualities of other people rather than simply to their group qualities' (1988:101).

Adorno *et al* (1950), Aboud (1988) and Brown (1998) see racism as one aspect of prejudice. Aboud considers the influence of parents, and also peers, on children's attitudes towards different ethnic groups (Aboud, 1988). I found that many children repeated views they had heard at home. Jeremy, a white boy from Bently school said, 'My dad says like errmm I'm not going to let you go to a mosque because it's not for your type and it's only Pakis that go and because my Dad doesn't like 'em.'

There is also a wider debate concerning children's 'in group/out group' identification (Tajfel and Turner, 1986), where children demonstrated prejudice towards groups to which they did not belong.

Experiencing racism

It is important to hear the voices of those who have experienced racism first hand and many feminist and Black scholars vividly describe their experiences. Women such as hooks (1992) and Hill Collins (1986); men such as Gilroy (1987) and Du Bois ([1903] 1989) are scholars who eloquently describe racism from a personal perspective. In *Representing Whiteness in the Black Imagination* (1992), hooks describes the terror she feels in the presence of white people. Her powerful personal style conveys what it is like to live in a white dominated world when one is not white. She uses the word 'terror' over a hundred times in her book (1992). She makes readers feel how it was, to be a child scurrying through a white populated area on the way to her grandma's house, and the terror instilled in black people by the presence of white people (hooks, 1992:344). She tells how, after giving a presentation on feminism and racism at the invitation of the Italian government, she was stopped and interrogated at the airport by white officials, who 'do not have to respond when I enquire as to why the questions they ask me are different from those asked of white people in the line before me' (1992:345).

Gilroy conveys the black experience of racism both academic and personal, and, like hooks, he uses language to powerful effect. In *There ain't no Black in the Union Jack* (1987) he explains the changing nature of racism which should be understood as a process:

> Bringing Blacks into history outside the categories of problem and victim and establishing the historical character of racism in opposition to the idea that it is an eternal or natural phenomenon depends on a capacity to comprehend political, ideological and economic change. (Gilroy,1987:27)

Gilroy argues that racist language used by tabloid newspapers fuels racism. These writers are not wanting 'race' to be ignored.

Jones found that student teachers in teacher education institutions in the UK stated they did not discriminate between children but that 'I see them as all the same' (Jones, 1999:140). He asserts that this refusal to acknowledge a child's cultural heritage is in fact a form of racism and I explore the concept of colour blindness later in this book. Daniel of

African heritage and Lucy of Asian heritage, both from Rarnlow school, discuss identity and friendship

> Daniel: There's a movie I watched that was made in 1951 and it's called Imitation of Life and it's about this girl and her mother's black, except when she was born she turned out to be white and she keeps on pretending she's white and ummm people abuse her because they find out that she's actually black – her family's black except she's white and she's embarrassed about that
>
> Sally: And what did you think about that when you watched that film?
>
> Daniel: I thought that umm [pause] you shouldn't be embarrassed about what colour you are
>
> Sally: Why do you think she felt she had to pretend that she was white?
>
> Daniel: Well mainly everyone she knew was white so she wanted to be like that
>
> Lucy: She probably didn't wanna be black but it doesn't matter what you are
>
> Daniel: Having friends it doesn't matter what colour you are it doesn't really matter – it matters about your personality really and what kind of friends you like to have

Two British white girls in Exforth school discuss a local event:

> Lisette: There was once a fight in a chip shop over black and white skin and black people aren't allowed in this country and that's what the fight was about ... [they are] allowed in this country I think it's a load of rubbish.
>
> Leah: I'm fine with black people in our country. IT'S A FREE COUNTRY! [Leah had written in capitals on her prompt sheet]
>
> Sally: When you say you're 'fine with black people in our country' do you think, for the black people who come and live in this country, it's their country as well, or is it still your country?
>
> Lisette: Well it's what they want it to be really they might want to like share the country with us sort of thing
>
> Sally: You don't agree June?
>
> June: No I don't think the British people want to share it but I think they'll allow them but not like make it their country.

Institutional racism

Key incidents have raised awareness of racism in the public domain and these often have an impact on the school community. The Macpherson Report (1999), which examined issues raised by the inquiry into the murder of black teenager Stephen Lawrence, illuminated the mistakes made by members of the Metropolitan police force who failed to treat the Lawrence family and Stephen's friend Duwayne Brooks appropriately (Brooks, 2003). The report discusses the mismanagement of events after the murder (Macpherson, 1999). Blair, Gillborn, Kemp and Macdonald (1999) discuss the report's influence and present the *Daily Mail's* headline 'Parents to blame' as an example of the misunderstanding of what institutional racism means. The Macpherson report is clear, however, that institutional racism is rife, defining it as:

> The collective failure of an organisation to provide an appropriate and profes-
> sional service to people because of their colour, culture, or ethnic origin. It
> can be seen or detected in processes, attitudes and behaviour which amount
> to discrimination through unwitting prejudice, ignorance, thoughtlessness
> and racist stereotyping which disadvantage ethnic minority people. (Mac-
> pherson, 1999:6.34)

The resources and displays in the school, my observation of lessons and interviews with staff and children revealed the 'institutional 'body language" (Dadzie, 2000:39) each school projected. How non racist and inclusive were they? Lewis (2005) found institutional racism in the schools she researched in America (also see chapter 8 of the present book).

Racism in Children's Lives

Troyna and Hatcher (1992) in England, and Lewis (2005) in America both use the term 'racialisation'. Troyna and Hatcher describe the aims of their study to understand 'the extent and ways in which the cultures of childhood may become racialised' (1992:49). 'Racialisation', as coined by Miles (1988), denotes:

> the political and ideological process by which particular populations are
> identified by direct or indirect reference to their real or imagined phenotypic
> characteristics in such a way as to suggest that the population can only be
> understood as a supposedly biological unity. (Miles, 1988:246)

In their examination of name-calling Troyna and Hatcher make the point that some children who use racist name-calling in fact hold racially egalitarian beliefs. They located racist name-calling within a typology (1992:76, fig 5.1). They argued that some racist name-calling is done by children who are not inherently racist but want to cause offence and hurt, and that this behaviour should be dealt with differently to those instances where children use racist language which expresses racist attitudes.

Troyna and Hatcher point out that interpretation of quantitative data about racist name-calling – now collected in all LAs under governmental directives – does not show whether it is racially motivated or used by non-racist children as a means of causing hurt. This important point strengthens Troyna and Hatcher's argument for research into race related issues to be qualitative rather than quantitative. It is one reason why I chose to use qualitative methods in my own research, and used small group interviews in which the children told me about their beliefs and experiences, as the following extracts show. Cassie and Saz are both white pupils at Exforth school.

> Cassie: I don't think it's like this country is just for white people and it's very rare to see like black people, I think it's just a country that we just like share
>
> Saz: Cos you can't claim that one spot of the earth is to be ours cos when we're going all over the place on holiday
>
> Cassie: I think we should have like more black people ... more white people in black areas and more black people in white areas ... then we'll get to know what they are like and it'll stop most wars
>
> Sally: has anyone talked to you about that?
>
> Cassie: I just seen all the stuff on TV about wars and stuff and murders of black people in Manchester and ...
>
> Sally: So you think people ought to get to know each other and then they wouldn't fight each other?
>
> Saz: People are all the same they've got umm the same hearts and that, everything's the same inside them it's just where they come from that gives them different skin colour

Louise, a white girl from Bently school, describes witnessing racist name-calling:

> Louise: Like umm last Friday I was going to the shop and there was this [Asian] person there and this boy Anthony and he turned around to him and called him a Paki
>
> Sally: And what did you do?

Louise: I just said Anthony stop being nasty to him cos you wouldn't like it if he was nasty to you

Sally: And what did Anthony say?

Louise: He just swore and went off

Sally: And how old's Anthony?

Louise: He's about 12

Sally: And do you know Anthony very well?

Louise: No but he's nasty and he beats people up.

Formative events and key racist incidents

Certain events have been influential in informing and shaping education and race today. Kincheloe and Steinberg's categories of multiculturalism (1997) are helpful in measuring 'degrees' of racism (see also chapter 5).

The Honeyford Affair

Halstead (1988) and Todd (1991) both identify the Honeyford affair as an example of racism at its worst. Roy Honeyford was a Bradford headteacher who disagreed with multicultural education and wrote an article to this effect in 1982. He called for immigrants to adapt to their new country, and said that schools should not be responsible for cultural maintenance as this was for parents to do. He argued that ethnic minority pupils should be taught 'British' culture and he disagreed with a critical approach to British history. He felt that underachievement by 'West Indian' [sic] children was due to the lack of encouragement by their parents (Todd, 1991:118).

Honeyford was suspended but then re-instated and finally took early retirement (Todd, 1991:118). His school roll fell by half and the affair was detrimental not only to pupils in his own school but to the whole education establishment as people came out in defence or opposition to Honeyford's opinions.

The affair polarised public opinion into pro-Honeyford groups who thought that a headteacher should be given the right to free speech, and anti-Honeyford groups who thought that Honeyford was a racist who fuelled the antagonism towards antiracist and multicultural education. In the conceptual framework of Kincheloe and Steinberg (1997) (see chapter 5), Honeyford can be placed as a conservative multiculturalist. Although there was some re-evaluation of multicultural education, several decades and more legislation later there is still concern about the achievement of Black children, and discrimination is still an issue.

The Murder of Ahmed Iqbal Ullah

Another catalytic event was the murder of 12 year old Ahmed Iqbal Ullah. Nayak argues that one of the possible motives for his killing by white classmate Darren Coulburn at Burnage school was a lack of attention to white ethnicity (Nayak, 1999:176). This reflects Kincheloe and Steinberg's left essentialist type of multiculturalism (1997). The implication is that the teaching at the school involved the promotion of Black culture and lifestyle and disparaged white culture. Troyna and Hatcher (1992:40) refer to a model they adapted from Waddington *et al* (1989) to support their view that the murder can be explained as not provoked by racialist motives yet at the same time described as a 'racist incident' – because of the 'racist culture and context' in which it took place (1992:41). The school had an antiracist policy but a policy does not in itself preclude racism (Dadzie, 2000).

Troyna and Hatcher's comment on the different layers of meaning which arise from the stabbing demonstrates that it was not a simple matter of a white boy being prejudiced against a Black boy. It was rather the culture of that setting – the school and community context. My conversation with boys at Deasham School shows that children today are aware of the subtleties of racism. Harry and Killik are white and Ashley is of Bangladeshi heritage.

> Harry: He [Roy, a Muslim boy identified by numerous children as a bully] calls white people names sometimes
>
> Sally: Oh right [pause] And what do you feel when that happens?
>
> Ashley: Miserable, embarrassed in front of Muslims
>
> Harry: Well it depends how he [Roy] uses the names – if he calls us *gora* well I think that actually in Asian that means 'whitie' they don't use it in a racist way so I think it depends how you use the word.
>
> Ashley: *Gora?*
>
> Harry: Like if you say somebody's Black you mean it in a racist way like you say 'blackie' or something to them – to umm be horrible because of their race that is racist but if you say they're Black just as

Kilik: Yeah just saying they're Black

Harry: Yeah not as an insult then I don't think it's racist.

The murder of Stephen Lawrence

The findings of the Macpherson Inquiry (1999) made it clear that the 'rotten apple' theory was not an acceptable explanation for the way the police dealt with the murder of Black teenager Stephen Lawrence. The report emphasised the institutional racism within public services as the main cause of the police's failure.

Blair *et al* (1999) consider the organisation of the curriculum to be at the heart of the problem. They criticise teachers who say they are willing in principle to discuss racism with children but do not make time to do so:

> Indeed the fetishisation of league tables and 'standards' measured by the crudest means possible actually provides exactly the circumstances where-by institutional racism flourishes. (Blair *et al*, 1999:9)

The Race Relations Amendment Act (2000) was the government's attempt to address some of the issues raised in the Report and yet many schools still fail to have a policy in place.

Multicultural Education

These key events together with others not discusses here, have been influential in the development of multicultural, intercultural, antiracist and citizenship education. Some see multicultural education as a failed endeavour (eg. Jones, 1998), whereas Figueroa (1995) Jackson (1997) and Brown (2008) are more positive about the benefits of multicultural education which has adapted and developed over time.

Much has happened in education since Figueroa and Jones wrote in the mid and late 1990s: in many schools funding has been allocated to support children in their learning, the ethnic minority and Traveller's achievement grant (EMTAG). Despite recent emphasis on the value of cultural diversity and the statutory requirement (Multiverse, 2009) to promote social cohesion, some schools still provide little opportunity for pupils to develop cultural awareness. Three white children from Exforth school told me.

> Steve: We don't do RE if it's sunny we do PE outside. In RE we watch a video of Islam, Buddha, allsorts. We watch the video and write down what we've watched

Bridget: RE stands for Religious Exercises. It's really boring. We watch videos and write stuff off sheets filling in the missing word about Pharaohs like Buddha

Kim: Not Pharaohs – that's history. We did symbols in religions, like the cross and the circle with dots in ying yang. I don't know ... I think it means peace. I know a lot about what we dream about.

The status of RE in both the predominantly white schools in my study differed from the multi-ethnic ones. Mrs Pink, a British white class teacher at Bently school stated, 'The quicker we can get RE done the quicker we can get to the ICT suite.'

An extract from this predominantly white school indicates the level of knowledge the children have:

Sally: Right so who would you describe as British white people – are there British white people in this school?

Michelle: Loads of them

Kurt: Yeah all the teachers are

Michelle: all the kids are

Kurt: I'm orange

Sally: What did you say?

Kurt: I'm orange

Sally: You're orange?

Bart: Looks like brown

Kurt: I'm half caste

Sally: What do you mean by half caste Kurt?

Kurt: Cos my mum – I think she's from Jamaica and errm and so that makes me half caste but I don't know what half caste means

Kurt seems reluctant to say he is either black or white. Perhaps this is because he is struggling with identity issues which, he acknowledges, he has not had an opportunity to discuss. Therefore he 'creates' an identity – 'orange'.

Learning about other cultures in school is not always a positive experience, as we hear from children at Rarnlow School. Alan is of Asian heritage, John and David are white.

Sally: So when you say school what kind of things do you learn at school?

John: In year 4 we did India

Alan: We did the Gurdwara

John: We talked about all the Indian people

Alan: And when we did Indian songs white people start laughing at us

John: Because sometimes we do PE and we did some Indian music too ... This lady was making a dance to do and everyone was laughing because it was stupid

David: It's like the Israel one and European dance and that woman started singing and everyone, nearly everyone in the class was laughing I was one that wasn't.

Citizenship in Education

Since the early 2000s Citizenship Education has been a statutory part of the National Curriculum. There was hope that it might foster inter-cultural and global understanding among pupils, but the preliminary report by Bernard Crick makes no reference to racism in society.

The Crick Report states:

> PSE, RE, moral education, whatever we call education specifically for values, are necessary but not sufficient conditions for good citizenship and good behaviour. (Crick, 1998:44)

But what is meant by 'good'? The suggestion is that teachers should be part of the process of 'delivering' a curriculum about 'being a good citizen,' yet the values of the teacher are taken for granted, as being pro democracy and pro being a 'good' citizen. The DfES guidance booklet and website, concerning the citizenship curriculum (2000, 2006b) out-line schemes of work for older children (Key Stage 3 and 4). These in-clude units such as 'Britain a Diverse society?' (unit 4) and 'Citizenship and RE: How do we deal with conflict?' (2006b). These units address issues concerning life in a multicultural and multi-ethnic society.

Darum acknowledges two dangers of indoctrination and values neutrality; there is a thin line between 'political education and political propaganda' (1998:21). I think this is what teachers find most difficult and, in my experience working with student teachers, there is often confusion between educating and indoctrinating, especially when teaching PSHE (Personal Social and Health Education). As Darum asserts 'the hidden curriculum is loaded with value messages, students 'inhale' them in their 12 years of schooling' (1998:23). This could be described in terms of institutional racism where teachers and the school ethos unwittingly convey racist messages. Darum asserts that the major message is 'be obedient to authority' (1998:25).

My research is located within the educational context as outlined above. I conclude this chapter with a summary of the rest of the book.

Organisation of the book

Chapter 1 argues that the context and educational climate in which the research was undertaken is value-laden but this is not always acknowledged. The evolution of multicultural/antiracist/intercultural and citizenship education has been driven by government, often responding to key events, as discussed. The complex concepts of culture and racism affect the lives of the children at school today and, as we have already seen, efforts to make them better informed have been less than successful.

Chapters 2 and 3 introduce the two predominantly white school, Exforth and Bently; and the two high proportion ethnic minority schools, Deasham and Rarnlow, where the research was undertaken. Discussion revolves around the hidden and formal curriculum and issues of diversity found within the schools.

In Chapter 4 the children explore their attitudes towards being British, and cultural identity. They talk about skin colour, about living and being born in Britain, and about speaking English.

Chapter 5 charts the stances adopted by the children in relation to those from a different culture, for example a position of colour blindness and ignoring differences (Jones, 1999), being politically correct and speaking or behaving to avoid offence (Modood, 2007:57), and white privilege – the dominance of white culture which thus favours white people and disadvantages Black and ethnic minority people (Kincheloe and Steinberg, 1997).

In Chapter 6 I present a systematisation of children's cultural awareness and explore the correlation between knowledge of different cultures and antiracist attitudes. Chapter 7 draws on my research and the literature to examine the possible influence of the school on children's cultural awareness. Here I outline the benefits and limitations of various approaches to multicultural and antiracist education. In the final chapter I present the implications of the research for policy and practice. My research methodology is described in the appendix.

2

Issues of diversity in two ethnically diverse schools

'It's good to see them get rid of their veils – it's a real release for them.' (Mr Millan, Deasham school)

This chapter discusses

■ the settings of the two multi-ethnic schools, Deasham and Rarnlow, and the reactions of staff to my research.

■ evidence of white privilege mindset in the two multi-ethnic schools

■ issues of diversity during lunchtimes, playtimes and in class

Deasham school – ethnically diverse, city location

Research into sensitive issues such as diversity and racism poses challenges for the researcher. Teachers and headteachers are not always keen to open their doors. On my first visit to Deasham school the headteacher, white, appeared keen to participate in the research. However the two Year 5 staff, also white, seemed less keen, sitting almost silent throughout our first discussion. The EMTAG (ethnic minority and Traveller achievement grant) teacher, himself of Pakistani heritage, spoke at length about his role. Data outlining the number of children in receipt of free school meals, those with English as an additional language, children's ethnic origin and the gender make up of the present Year 5 cohort, were compiled in the summer when the children were still in year 4. The data illustrates the high proportion of Pakistani (42%) and Indian heritage children (27%) compared with white (16%), African-Caribbean (3%) and others (11%) (these statistics relate to how parents choose to describe their particular heritage). The majority of the Pakistani heritage children were Muslim and the Indian heritage children were mostly Sikh.

Deasham is a city school set amidst well-established red brick terraced housing inhabited predominantly by British Asians. The building is Victorian with some modern extensions. There is a large playground surrounded by small grassy areas and a pleasant seated area amongst trees. The school is a large primary with 475 on roll which increased to 520 in the Summer of 2001 when the new children joined reception. In the Year 5 cohort of 74 children 18 (24%) were in receipt of free school meals. Fifty three children (72%) spoke English as an additional language and the most common first language spoken was Gujerati. There were 39 girls (53%) and 35 boys (47%) in year 5. This was a school which had a rich cultural mix.

The opening welcome page in Deasham school's prospectus for parents was written in English and Gujerati, and the headteacher stressed the vital role played by parents and the school in their child's education,

> The more we work towards a partnership of learning, the more your children will enjoy school and be successful in school. (Deasham school prospectus page 4)

White privilege mindset in a multi-ethnic school

Celebration of diversity and commitment to social cohesion were apparent – the headteacher, Mrs Winter was obviously dedicated to promoting antiracism and she believed Ofsted to be unaware of the complex issues faced by pupils with English as an additional language. Yet despite her commitment, evidence suggested that even in this positive multi-ethnic school there was still a white privilege mindset, especially amongst the white teachers – the majority.

I had thought I would find it difficult to build up a relationship with Mr Millan, one of the year 5 teachers, because he remained silent at the first meeting. But he proved to be an open and caring teacher. When I first arrived in Mr Millan's class, he was keen to tell me about the make-up of the group and how the school had changed over the 23 years he had been there. Mr Millan described Deasham school's intake when he first began teaching there, as: '50% African Caribbean, 30% white, 20% Asian mainly Sikh. Now it's mostly Muslim and Sikh with very few African Caribbean. Now it's mainly mixed race.'

Mr Millan said that the top group in Deasham school would probably be the middle group in other schools. He said the whites were: 'mainly from one parent families – that's why they are here.'

I interpreted this to mean Mr Millan was suggesting that the white children at Deasham school were on the whole less intelligent than white children in other schools and that he thought that the whole cohort of children, both white and ethnic minority, were less intelligent than a cohort in a predominantly white school. Throughout my stay at Deasham school Mr Millan struck me as a conscientious and friendly teacher who encouraged all his students, especially those who had an aptitude for sport, which was his passion. He made comments about the children's ability and ethnicity which pointed to his constant need to rank children in some way, sometimes negatively.

One day one child from Mr Millan's class returned after an extended visit to Pakistan. Mr Millan greeted the child with the comment: 'You are looking well. Lost some weight? Usually do when you go away. Were you poorly?'

While well meaning, I believe Mr Millan was inadvertently sending out implicit messages that when British Asian children return to the country of their heritage, the expectation is that they will not fare as well in this culture. Thus there may be a belief in the privilege of the English as opposed to the Pakistani lifestyle. The expectation is that in this country you thrive, whereas in Pakistan you are poorly, grow thin and do not thrive. Yet this perception may well have been endorsed by the children themselves because on the journey to and from the local museum (during an out of school visit), several British Asian children of Pakistani heritage were talking about life in Pakistan and how their teachers were cruel and threw chalk and board rubbers at them. Another child, Carlo, admitted that his family owned a huge house in Pakistan and yet in this country they lived in a small terraced home.

Mr Millan was subject leader for Physical Education (PE) and was strict during these lessons. He commented that the more able worked on the right hand side, the less able on the left. After Tazia and Zoe (both

British Muslim girls) had changed for PE, Mr Millan remarked that Tazia was one of the best athletes and how good it was to 'get rid of the veils – it's a real release for them'.

Thus with his white privilege mindset (discussed in chapters 4 and 5) he sees these girls in terms of athletes who were being held back by their religion, which, to him, was not as important as sport.

Mrs Moser, the other Year 5 teacher, also white, was a member of the Senior Management Team. She too was dedicated and hardworking but displayed a similar mindset. Her attitude was encapsulated in an incident when Melissa, an African Caribbean girl, came in late while she was in mid-flow in a literacy lesson. When Mrs Moser reprimanded her, Melissa whispered to a friend and was immediately asked to sit at the front. She accidentally knocked into a bin because she was cramped, and the teacher promptly asked whether she wanted to stay in at lunch-time. Melissa was described by both Mr Millan and Mrs Moser as a 'troublemaker' and their expectations for her to act as such reinforced their assumptions. Mr Millan described her as 'a right pain. The children have to take it in turns to have her on their table.'

Connolly (1998) has noted teachers' behaviour towards African Caribbean children they stereotyped (see also Sewell, 2000). In Deasham school, the stereotyping was hardly excessive but I saw a few isolated incidents where the teachers' expectations were not value-free and a white western mindset dominated.

Lunchtimes and playtimes at Deasham school

The headteacher was committed to promoting different cultures and employed many ethnic minority staff. The school had opted out of Local Authority (LA) school lunches and the catering team made their own food so they could offer dishes from different cultures. On a day when I visited the school, a 'Vaisaki special' dhal dish was on the menu. The children I sat with at lunch were articulate and lunchtime was a social event: the atmosphere was happy and relaxed and the children chatted to each other and the staff. There were, unusually for schools, vases of flowers on the tables. The atmosphere was of an enjoyable social event rather than an activity to be finished as painlessly and quickly as possible – as I saw at lunchtime in Exforth, a predominantly white school discussed in the next chapter.

26

One lunchtime I sat next to Ahmed who told me about Allah and the Devil:

> if you kill a spider you get punished ... if you go to heaven you get what you want, for example playstations! Whereas if you go to hell you get burnt and come alive again, get burnt and come alive again.

Ahmed accepted that non-adherence to Muslim rules was sometimes permissible. For he explained that he had: 'an injection [grommet] in my ears and am not allowed to wash or go swimming but I know that Allah wouldn't punish me for that because I couldn't help it!'

When I began relating this to Mrs Moser and another teacher in the staffroom, they knew exactly who I was talking about and said knowingly that his father was 'even worse.' I felt this implied that proselytising, especially for Islam, was not viewed in a positive light.

Playtimes were well organised with numerous resources available for the children, such as skipping ropes, stilts and hoops. Mr Millan played music tapes for the children to listen to. Children could hire small play equipment such as bats and balls. This organised play ensured that the children were usually well engaged, so not bored.

While out on the playground children came to chat with me. Melissa told me:

> I enjoy English and Maths. My best friend's Alison and my second is Sarah. I think this school is very good – where's this actually going?
>
> Sally: Eventually into a book if my examiners are pleased with it!
>
> Melissa: Will it be sold – in W.H Smiths or somewhere?
>
> Jason: That's the first time she's been interested in books!

On another occasion Melissa asked me if her teacher would be reading what I had written. I explained that I would be presenting a feedback report to teachers and children but that everyone would have a pseudonym and so teachers would not be able to identify particular children's comments (David *et al*, 2001). Melissa seemed genuinely concerned about this, and as I spent more time at the school, I got the impression that she did not always feel comfortable with her class teacher. I did not think it appropriate to ask her directly whether she had a problem with Mr Millan or felt he acted in a racist way towards her, but I thought her body language and a few of her comments suggested this was the case.

Inclusive assemblies

Observing assemblies often provided rich data because headteachers use them to communicate their philosophy. Much teaching and learning about culture, lifestyle choices and other citizenship issues take place during assembly time so they are a good indicator of the ethos of the school. This was certainly the case in Deasham school. Mrs Winter was keen to stress that a healthy mind and body are to be prized and she spoke about this in an assembly where she promoted the Fruit Scheme, which was introduced and funded by the government in 2002, and ensured that every child in infant classes was provided with a piece of fresh fruit each day with a view to encouraging children to develop healthy eating habits. She said: 'Of all the things that you might own the one thing that is totally yours is your body. It remains yours and changes with you. You need to help it to be healthy.'

This was during an inclusive assembly. The school had a dispensation granted by the local SACRE (Standing Advisory Council for RE), which lifted the legal requirement for the acts of collective worship to be 'mainly or wholly of a broadly Christian nature' (McCreery *et al*, 2008: 15). There was no prayer during this assembly.

However, another assembly led by an ethnic minority teacher, Mr Hanif was less inclusive. Mr Hanif began with a Sikh greeting which he expected the many Sikh children to respond with. When they did not, he asked if they were ashamed of saying it. Next, he discussed the festivities surrounding May Day. He was responsible for conducting assemblies about various festivals, such as Id-Ul-Fitr, Christmas, Vaisaki. He talked about Maypole dancing and young girls getting up early to wash their faces in the dew. While Mr Hanif had researched into festivals and collected some interesting information, his account did not touch on the inner meaning of festivals (see McCreery *et al*, 2008). The Sikh children seemed embarrassed by Mr Hanif's Sikh greeting and even more by his admonishment. The assembly was well-meaning but merely reenforced stereotypical thinking rather than challenging it: few indigenous English people wash their faces in the morning dew and join in Maypole dancing. Mr Hanif had been appointed to address issues of diversity and he was obviously featuring different cultures in his assemblies. But just because an assembly is led by an ethnic minority teacher does not ensure that issues of diversity will be appropriately addressed and stereotyping and racism challenged.

Curriculum issues

One of the subjects I looked at in all four schools was Religious Education (RE) because this gave me a good idea of the status given to cultural and religious issues. It was covered in different ways in each school and also perceived differently by different children.

At Deasham RE was taught mainly through study days held once or twice a term, Deasham school's RE policy states: 'RE is not taught separately but rather as an integral part of topic work'. All classes abandoned their usual timetabled lessons for the study day and children were sometimes mixed in year groups to work with teachers on a theme related to RE, such as festivals like Divali, Christmas, Eid and Vaisakhi. Teachers could choose a festival to study from a comprehensive list. The aim is to encourage: 'understanding and tolerance of each other's customs and beliefs' (Deasham School Policies Handbook, p14).

When Mr Millan taught an RE lesson during my visit, he wrote the words 'Belief' and 'Conviction' on the board and explained that 'what someone believes in is accepted as true, for example, Wayne might believe Man United are the best, but he never was a good judge!' He gave out a photocopied sheet which asked the children to rank several statements in order of importance (Gent and Gent, 1997:115). Several children wrote 'People should believe in God' in the top three. Next came 'Old people should be cared for by their families', followed by 'Drinking and driving is wrong'. Many children ranked low or not at all that, 'Men and women should have the same opportunities'. Mr Millan commented that 'boys and girls are treated fairly but in some lives that might not be the same. Some girls are not allowed to go swimming – isn't that right Zoe and Kate?' [two Muslim girls].

The girls wore the hijab and Mr Millan was intimating that in Muslim culture there is gender inequality. His comments may have been well-intended but they reflected his prejudice that Muslim culture is inferior to Western culture because of the subjugation of women within some communities. He failed to mention the importance Islam places on the role of the woman as mother. He was judging Islam from his own Western standpoint which, he implied, was the correct one.

The RE co-ordinator in Deasham school, Mr Modood, of Pakistani heritage, talked about RE in the school. He made it clear that the children were not actually celebrating the festivals in a religious way; rather that during the study days they learnt about the festivals celebrated in different cultures. He described his role as 'public relations rather than study skills manager'.

This certainly contrasts with most RE co-ordinators, who see themselves as curriculum leaders. Mr Modood saw himself as a mediator between the faith communities, and the school, which was made up of mainly white staff and governors. The staffroom was frequented mostly by the white staff, the ethnic minority staff were rarely seen there. Mr Modood stressed the importance of his role as mediator between the school and the community especially over: 'misunderstandings between the public and the school'.

He cited a case where some Muslim parents opposed their children attending the local church for a school event. Mr Modood interceded by contacting these parents. That year the children were engaged in a musical event to be performed at the church and few parents objected, whereas the previous year Mr Modood told me that 'nine parents still said no but that was more about a problem with the teacher'. He was unwilling to elaborate on this situation – maybe he was being discreet.

Mr Modood said that in the past they used to study only Vaisakhi, Divali, Eid and Christmas but this year Shabbat and Easter had been added, to give teachers more flexibility as some had wanted to explore another religion. He said that when he started at Deasham school, ten years before, there was a fear of causing offence. He said staff felt that 'if we do an assembly about Sikhism and we make a mistake we'll probably annoy somebody'.

He stressed that the children were learning about religion and that 'we are not trying to convert'. Mrs Moser, in whose classroom the discussion was taking place, was obviously half-listening and interjected, 'we have too many study days'. Mr Modood replied that study days were part of the normal educational planning. He mentioned the close liaison he had with members of an organisation in the city which provided cultural workshops and visits to local places of worship in the city. After he left her classroom, Mrs Moser remarked: 'There are more study days than we used to have and it got boring'.

She liked the introduction of Judaisim. She felt confident about teaching on the study days and she liked the fact that there was 'no recording – the work was mostly for display and so there was not so much pressure'.

From a pedagogical perspective I believe that the lack of assessment in RE lowers the status of the subject.

Rarnlow school – ethnically diverse pupils, city location

During my first visit to Rarnlow school Mrs Gardon, the white headteacher, indicated she was keen to participate in the research. Mrs Singh, of Punjabi heritage, and Mr Denton, white, were equally positive. Mrs Gardon spoke with pride about Rarnlow school's recent successes in Ofsted inspections and benchmarking exercises but added that she did not want the school to become complacent especially about the achievement or support of ethnic minority children, saying that 'there are pockets where we could improve'.

She told me that the area in which the school was located was 'challenging – we have aggressive parents and the Indian heritage parents are learning how to be fighters, they are caught up in the *mêlée*'.

Mrs Gardon appeared committed to multicultural education and had been involved in an earlier project to promote multicultural awareness but this had since ceased: 'There *has* been good practice but then it fell apart. I worked with people from the university but they all left to take up other posts and it fell apart.'

She mentioned another school in the city with a high proportion of ethnic minority children but where 'there is no support for the Indian children. There is very little training and the teachers are unaware of the rich culture. I fear that these communities will loose their heritage. Some of the Indian women are being isolated.' She talked about initiatives in her own school, which did address the needs of the community and reported that the EMTAG and RE co-ordinator had been on long term sick leave and a new RE co-ordinator had taken over the roles.

Rarnlow Junior school is located in the midst of a 1960s housing estate in a part of the city which is not affluent. Built in 1970s, it is spacious and well maintained. The playground is rather small for the number of children in the school, but there is a large adjacent field where the children were allowed to play on dry days. A seated area close to the school has a few benches arranged around a couple of small trees. There were 285 children on roll: 21 per cent Indian, 11 per cent African Caribbean, 2 per cent Pakistani and Bangladeshi and 66 per cent white. The language most commonly spoken other than English was Punjabi. Most of the ethnic minority children were Sikh, with a few Muslim and Hindu children. Cultural and RE events were given high profile and the Governor's report noted the celebration of major religious festivals which are built into the school calendar.

The school also hosted Religious Education workshops and had local church links and a weekly Christian lunchtime club open to all pupils. Concerts in school included Indian dance and steel pan. The school prospectus articulated a conviction to develop and maintain home/ school partnership and links with the community. Rarnlow school had been recognised as An Investor in People.

There were various differences between Rarnlow and Deasham school. Rarnlow school's prospectus stated the recommended school dress in the uniform policy section. The children of Asian heritage did not wear shalwar kameez but sweatshirts, tops and trousers, or skirts in the school colours. As a visitor I was struck by the regulated nature of the children at Rarnlow school. I saw no girl or female teacher of Asian heritage wearing the hijab, although there was no ban on wearing it, and the dress code was Western. However, this may have been somewhat insensitive to the religious and cultural background of the pupils and their families. In contrast to Deasham school, Rarnlow school's prospectus was written in English only, which was surprising given Mrs Gardon's commitment to a multicultural ethos.

Favourites – relationships between staff and children
Racism can be linked with a culture of domination and bullying so I was interested in the relationships between the adults and children. Domination starts with favouring one person over another and in Rarnlow school I saw examples of favouritism, albeit from a caring and hardworking teacher (Elton-Chalcraft, 2008a).

Mr Denton, a white teacher with responsibility for Science, arranged his classroom in a traditional way, with pairs of children sitting at desks facing the board. I sat next to a white girl on my first visit, and she told me her name, Charlene, was unusual. Her friend Arvinder, who is of Asian heritage, said that her name was unusual too – the girls cited white Western names such as Susan, Alice and Rachel as 'normal'.

Mr Denton had a good relationship with many of the children and joked with them. I gained the impression that he had 'favourites' and gave these children extra time to work out answers. Rosanne, a white girl, was often singled out by him as being 'annoying.' During a history lesson he said: 'Rosanne you are beginning to irritate me. Look at me! If you only have silly things to say be quiet'.

During a music lesson in Mr Denton's class, children on the right side of the class dominated the discussion about tempo and style of music after listening to some excerpts from a CD. Terri especially became very animated and called out several times. But when Rosanne called out an answer she was reprimanded by Mr Denton: 'You are really beginning to annoy me Rosanne Smith'.

I think he must have realised what I was thinking, as he looked at me and stated 'The people over here, although over excited, have some-thing to say which is relevant'.

I was not convinced. The teacher has a crucial role in promoting self esteem and their expectations have an effect on children's achievement (Arthur *et al*, 2006). Rosanne remained silent for the rest of the lesson, while Terri continued to shout out answers exuberantly and be praised by Mr Denton.

Mrs Singh, a teacher of Punjabi heritage, had a calm and friendly manner with the children. Unlike Mr Denton, she organised the tables in her classroom for interactive group work. While being supportive of Mrs Singh, Mrs Gardon nevertheless gave me the impression that this teacher was under great pressure, saying:

> She commutes from M town [40 miles away]. She moved in the middle of term and also had a week off for a traditional arranged marriage. She lives with his family. This all happened the week before Ofsted! Also she had a car crash – I think it was, in part, due to the pressure she was under.

But Mrs Gardon was full of praise for Mr Denton: 'Oh he'll go far. He's well known to the Science advisors and will probably not be at this school long. He's young but up and rising.' I felt that she had different expectations for these two teachers which could be related to issues of ethnicity and also gender.

Lunchtimes and playtimes – equality issues

Most playtimes I was surrounded by curious children. The children played well despite the smallness of the playground. Both boys and girls talked to me about which Upper school they wanted to attend. They had ranked the schools according to reputation and one child's family had moved house in order to be in the catchment area of a school deemed to be good. A bad school was summed up as one where bullies were unchallenged and the GCSE results were not good.

Another topic of conversation at playtime revolved around the plans for an extension to the playground. Rarnlow had a school council which Lucy, of Asian heritage, described: 'We talk about what needs changing. I used to be on it before – I can't remember when. We have to talk about what would make things better.'

So the children were involved in making decisions about their environment and to some degree about other matters too. It is interesting that Rarnlow, Deasham and Bently schools all had school councils and I felt that all had a more equal relationship between children and staff and less bullying, aggression amongst the children at playtimes and lunchtimes than Exforth school did. Exforth was in the process of setting up a school council.

Lunchtime was a civilised affair at Rarnlow, with orderly lines and children sitting in the well-lit and ventilated hall to eat packed lunches or school dinners. I was not aware of halal food being on offer. Conversation was allowed and some of the Sikh children were keen to tell me about their home life and how they celebrated festivals like Vaisakhi. Such festivals were sometimes mentioned in assemblies.

Assemblies at Rarnlow school

Mrs Tejpreet, the newly-appointed RE subject leader, told me that on the whole the assemblies were based around Christian festivals but that other festivals from Islam, Sikhism and Hinduism were mentioned.

Unlike Deasham school, Rarnlow was not exempt from the requirement to make assemblies 'wholly, broadly or mainly Christian' (Teece, 2001).

In one assembly, Mr Minden, the deputy headteacher warned the children about the cramped dimension of the playground and asked for them to take care. He told a story about name-calling. The story concerned Mohammed Ali, the famous boxer. As a child, he ran to his mother at the end of school to complain that children had been teasing him. They had told him that Black people did not get to heaven because there were no pictures of black cherubs in photographs the teacher had been showing to the class. Ali's mother replied 'who do you think was taking the pictures?'

Mr Minden used this story to advise the children to think about the victim's response to name-calling. If the recipient feels hurt by it even if it was not meant cruelly, it is still wrong. He did not explore why neither the teacher in the story nor Ali's mother showed the class images of black angels. During this assembly there was no prayer. Children were being asked not to misbehave but, unlike at Deasham school, no strategies were actually used to engage them usefully to prevent trouble occurring. During my visit a few children talked to me about bullying but I did not witness any incidents in the playground.

Another assembly was based around the Muslim festival of Eid Mubarak. Mrs Gardon talked about Mrs Tejpreet who celebrated this festival because she was Muslim and remarked that her parents had been on the Hajj, the pilgrimage to Mecca (Fisher, 2002). Some children were dressed in the Muslim cap and white robe during the assembly. Mrs Gardon concluded the assembly by saying: 'We celebrate all religions. We should wish Muslim children 'Happy Eid' when they return to school'. The assembly was informative and respectful. At the end Mrs Gardon read the Muslim call to prayer and invited children to 'Bow your head and if you agree with this you can say Amen'.

I felt that Mrs Gardon had tried in the assembly to be inclusive, acknowledging the Muslim festival and respecting some of her Muslim pupils' absence to celebrate it at home. She was well-meaning in her stance towards the prayer but 'Amen' is a Christian term. She told the assembled children that there would be no song today as she felt it was inappropriate. I surmised that it would have been taken from *Come and*

Praise (Coombes and Taylor, 1988) which is a Christian hymn book used in many primary schools: the children from Rarnlow school sang songs from it during hymn practice assemblies which took place once a week.

I attended one of the hymn practice assemblies and despite a lack of leadership from the two teachers at the front, the children sang loudly and in tune. The teachers had to take it in turns to lead hymn practice whether or not they had musical talent. All five hymns were either explicitly or implicitly Christian and so unsuitable for Muslim, Sikh, Hindu or agnostic or atheist children.

Some of the less able children were taken out of assemblies for extra work with the special needs teacher, so were denied the input about Eid Mubarak. One white boy in the less able group showed some awareness of differences between Muslims, Hindus and Sikhs, but was confused: 'We've done about Sikhs but I don't think they're [Muslims and Sikhs] the same. The Muslims pray in a gurdwara.'

Another white boy said that 'Sikhs have got quite a lot of gods'. This is a possible confusion with Hindus, many of whom consider the one supreme Brahman to have many manifestations – though not separate Gods in their own right, another misunderstanding of the Hindu conception of God. Most Sikhs believe in one 'God' (Fisher, 2002).

A white girl said '[Muslims] go to mosque, they need to have a special wash ... I knew that before, we had an assembly about it before.'

Another assembly revolved around the celebration of children's work. Mrs Gardon looked carefully at several folders of work about the ancient Romans. The children were praised for the care they had taken and I felt that all the work was being genuinely admired and raising the children's self esteem.

Curriculum issues

The children had mixed feelings about RE. Gurdeep said ' I hate RE, it's boring with Mr Denton.' Other children joined in and Lucy (of Asian heritage but who chose a western pseudonym) said that they had discussed Islam. Manpreet (Asian heritage) said 'the last time we did RE it was about pulse rate'. She was corrected by Lucy: 'No that was Science'. Manpreet defended her ignorance – 'I didn't know that because I went to India'.

I had a discussion with Mrs Tejpreet, the RE co ordinator. She had only recently taken this role yet her skills had been recognised by the city RE advisor who asked her to contribute to the updating of the local Agreed Syllabus for RE. She had begun to devise and introduce a comprehensive scheme of work based on the local Agreed Syllabus for RE and also particular units from QCA material. She had also written the recently ratified RE policy for Rarnlow school.

Mrs Tejpreet explained that she did not see herself as an expert and that the teachers were fully responsible for planning their individual lessons but that she was in charge of the resources and could be called upon for support. She mentioned that the music curriculum included music from a variety of cultures.

A white educational co-worker, Mrs Smart, worked regularly with the two Year 5 classes. One of her duties was to take a small number of children to the hall where they engaged in activities from a book about circle time (Mosely, 1996, 1998). Although I found these sessions of unburdening positive on the whole, because they built up children's self esteem, I had concerns about their other effects. The children were asked personal questions and when I took part I felt uncomfortable about sharing information. The children were asked what animal they were most like and this would offer an indication of their values – for example one child said 'I am like a monkey because I like playing tricks'.

Mrs Smart meant well but she assumed an authoritative role in these sessions about what behaviour was right or wrong. However, it was a good team building strategy because the children were encouraged to be positive about one another. Mrs Smart had told me that this activity had been started so as to encourage Rachel, of dual heritage white and African Caribbean background, to get along with the other children. Rachel tried hard to be sensitive to her partner's needs. On the whole, the teacher's attitudes towards Rachel were more positive than Mr Millan's strategies in Deasham school with Melissa, who was of Caribbean heritage and who, like Rachel, had been described as presenting challenging behaviour.

Mrs Card, a peripatetic teacher (white), came in to school to teach steel pan to groups of children. Rarnlow had a set of steel pans which had been donated by the upper school. She described the history of steel pans and spoke positively about Caribbean culture. The children and I thoroughly enjoyed the session, although not every child was given the chance to play. This much pilloried form of 'multiculturalism' has a place in schools like Rarnlow, that are trying to address racism.

A literacy lesson taken by Mrs Singh was fascinating. The text was about a traditional Asian family with a Grandpa Chatterjee who wears a *dhoti*, a length of cloth traditionally worn by males. This family was visited by Grandpa Leicester, who wears Western clothes and is highly respected and somewhat feared by the family. At the end of the story Grandpa Leicester works with Grandpa Chattergee to make lunch and he joins him in wearing a *dhoti*. I realise the focus of the lesson was on literacy but Mrs Singh could have used the story to explore some cultural issues. For example, were the family afraid of Grandpa Leicester because he wore a suit, was rich, did not like mess, or because he had an authoritative character? Was his Western style of dress part of this authority? What did the children think about his wearing the *dhoti*?

Mrs Singh could have talked about her own experiences of Western versus Asian culture. But perhaps she thought that this was inappropriate or did not want to talk about personal matters. She told me that the children at Rarnlow school were familiar with the Asian words in the story like *dhoti*.

The children were positive about the story and when I asked them about some of the issues, Deepak, of Asian heritage, and Graham, a white boy showed their awareness that normal was a relative concept. During a discussion about some of the names in the story being 'funny' Graham said:

> It's different to our stories because it's got funny names ... but it might not be funny to them. But people who's not in their illition [tradition] ... but it's funny for us ... anyone can come in this country, some people from China can come over here.

Graham's comments show some acknowledgement of and tolerance towards other people's cultures. We see this also in many interviews discussed in the next chapter. In the plenary Mrs Singh asked the children to think of the words which had been unfamiliar to them and asked them to think of terms from other cultures which are now commonplace in British culture, such as the Italian pizza. This went some way to develop children's awareness. But this task was based on a Western perspective, as the familiarity of the words was judged against a white British perspective. For example the word *dhoti* would not have been unfamiliar to a British Asian. Mrs Singh set a homework task for the children to write down ten words from another culture and identify the country of origin. When this homework came in a few days later the majority of children referred to foods such as:

burgers – USA
pitta bread – Greece
hot dogs – America
curry – India
kebab – Greece
sugar – Jamaica
tea – China

This was hardly informative and the children had stereotyped the various cultures. Mrs Singh said that because she had used pizza as an example they had latched on to this. This is an example of a well mean-ing activity which in fact re-enforced stereotypes. I found it ironic that this homework was set by an ethnic minority teacher who had become conditioned by Western perspectives.

I later observed an RE lesson about Judaisim taken by Mrs Singh. I was impressed with her re-cap of the children's previous learning and her willingness to talk about her own faith. She asked 'Is there a rule which says we must follow a particular religion? ... I'm a Sikh but I don't have to believe in just Sikhism.'

Mrs Singh promoted a climate of openness and the children were en-couraged to learn 'about' and 'from' religion (the two key attainment targets set out in the locally agreed syllabus for RE by Derbyshire County Council in 1999). Mrs Singh drew out the similarities between the Sikh Guru Granth Sahib and the Torah scroll, saying: 'You won't be able to understand it. I think it's [written from] right to left. That's how we do. It's also like the Guru Granth Sahib because it gets covered.'

Mrs Singh mentioned Jewish artefacts and the children discussed similarities between religions, such as the use of symbols. She referred to other learning, for example that the star of David had been men-tioned in an assembly about Anne Frank. She encouraged discussion throughout the lesson but the task was not challenging, because the children were asked to copy chunks of material from the board next to the correct picture on their worksheet.

I observed a swimming lesson at Ranlow, which raised some interesting issues. The city leisure centre had introduced changing room facilities in response to requests from the community. For example there were changing rooms for:

> Female child with male parent
> Female child with female parent
> Male child with female parent
> Male child with male parent.

However it was noticeable that most children of Asian heritage, especially the girls, were in the lower groups for swimming and many of them told me their mothers never swam or did not drive, so never went to the swimming pool with them. Some of these girls were modest in the changing rooms. Although none of the children referred to this at the time, I believe that they noticed it.

Another interesting issue concerned Rachel, of white and African Caribbean background. A white boy, Jason, on seeing Rachel emerge from the girl's changing room remarked loudly to his friends: ' Rachel looks like she's been electrocuted – look at her hair!' Rachel had removed the band from her thick black hair. She looked upset and said 'everyone picks on me, it's annoying me.'

Interestingly, an African Caribbean girl, Annie, who had similar hair, waited until she was in the privacy of her seat on the bus before removing her band. I wondered if this was intentional. The teasing of Rachel continued on the bus,

> Bill: Rachel you look like a lion.

> Rachel: Gosh I hate my hair, it's annoying, everybody calls me names.

Rachel seemed to be ashamed of her appearance and directed her anger at her hair rather than at the insensitivity of the children who were teasing her. Annie, too, seemed embarrassed about her hair, preferring to comb it in private, away from the glance of the children. The teacher in charge seemed not to notice the teasing and did not intervene. I found it hard to stay silent but I wanted to maintain my 'least adult' role (see appendix).

Mr Denton led a lesson about the Aztecs, where the discussion centred around fact and opinion. Mr Denton told the class that the Aztecs sacrificed humans by tearing out their hearts. Everyone gasped, 'How cruel'. He went on to explain that that had been the response of his teachers when he was at school but that now he wanted the children to consider why the Aztecs did this and he explained: 'They thought that the sun would not rise if they didn't sacrifice.'

The children came to the conclusion that in the European's opinion this act was barbaric but to the Aztecs it was acceptable. Raymond called out: 'The Aztecs did it because it's their religion.' The children who had been interviewed by me smiled at me and called out, 'their culture!'

Terri's comment was interesting: 'We're on the Aztec's side because we're doing about the Aztecs. But really we should be on the European's side'. And it was perceptive because she was aware that facts are interpreted from different perspectives. But also she considered her own perspective and engaged with the debate with reference to her own identity. Thus she was involving herself in the debate rather than taking on the role of neutral observer. Clearly, she understood the notion of opinion.

Mr Denton discussed the fact that we no longer hold such erroneous views because we are better informed: 'Now we have computers and TV we know pretty much what others are like.' He and Toxic discussed the origin of skin colour, deducing that the nearer to the equator the darker the skin but that people with dark skins who come to live near the North pole do not suddenly become white.

The discussion moved to the domination of one culture over another and the enforcement of Christianity on the dwindling Aztec population. Mr Denton stated:

> History isn't just fact. It's usually one group of people telling others what to do ... What's good for one group you can bet is not good for another.

I asked individual children about what they thought about one culture, such as the Spaniards, imposing their religion and culture onto another group, the Aztecs. Toxic, of dual white and African Caribbean heritage said:

> The Spanish made the Aztecs be Christian ... the Aztecs were living happily with their own religion. The Spanish made them believe in Christianity because nearly the whole of Europe believed in Christianity, so they thought they'd make the whole world believe in Christianity. The Spanish believed in the one and only God called God. They wanted to try to stop them breaking one of the commandments – don't kill. I think that was a good idea ... South Americans turned into strong Christians.

I asked Toxic why the Aztecs did not refuse to turn to Christianity. He said: 'Because they wanted to live on. They were down to two million, so they probably just went along with it.' Toxic had told me in the taped interview that he was a strong Christian, and so I asked him if his own Christian belief had made a difference to the way he looked at the story. He replied:

> Not really, because the Aztecs had their own religion and they were happy with it. If I was [had been] an Aztec I would have p ... disagreed, protested. I wouldn't mind if I got killed I'd protest to keep my religion. I wouldn't let anyone do that [force me to convert].

Thus, despite being a strong adherent of Christianity, Toxic was able to put himself in the shoes of the Aztecs and empathise with their loyalty to their religion.

I asked Terri about this issue, and she replied, 'I don't think anybody should be persuaded to change their beliefs, even sacrifice, if they believe in it ... But I wouldn't have liked to have lived in those times.'

I wondered whether Mr Denton's politically correct presentation of Aztecs as being the injured party had influenced the children's interpretations. Certainly Terri had questioned this. But many of the Asian heritage children felt sympathetic towards the Aztecs. As Manpreet said:

> You really should follow your own religion ... You should pray to your own God, He's given you everything ... Now[adays] we've got one God. Say I'm a Sikh and you're a Christian, we would all have one God. Christians have Jesus and Sikhs have Guru Nanak. I'm not quite sure [about Hindus] they have Rama and Sita – I'm not Hindu.

Most said they did not think it was fair to force the Aztecs to abandon their culture and religion. Clearly, the children had a sense of justice.

3

Character and ethos of two predominantly white schools

RE stands for Religious exercises. It's really boring. We watch videos and write stuff off sheets filling in the missing word about Pharaohs like Buddha. (Lara, white girl, Exforth school)

This chapter considers

■ the settings of the two predominantly white schools, Exforth and Bently, including the reactions of staff to my research

■ evidence of cultures of dominance and the white western mindset in predominantly white schools

■ issues of diversity during lunchtimes, playtimes and during curriculum time

Exforth school – predominantly white, on the outskirts of town

Exforth school had had a series of headteachers and acting headteachers and this affected the ethos of the school and particularly behaviour. It also had an effect on the collection of data and reporting of results. During my initial visit I met the acting headteacher Mr Penny and two Year 5/6 teachers. When I commenced my research six months later, a new acting headteacher had been appointed on a temporary basis, Mr Hans a headteacher from another school in the county. Mr Penny had returned to his post of Year 5/6 teacher. When I wanted to return to the school to present my interim report, a new headteacher Mr Chalk, had been appointed but he could not offer me a time to visit the school and discuss the interim report with the children and staff.

Most staff were committed and professional but the original head-teacher's long-term sick leave had had a detrimental effect. Mr Hans informed me that although the state of children's awareness of cultural diversity and the delivery of Religious Education were causes for concern, it was more important to put other systems in place which had been neglected. He told me: 'PSHE and RE are important but are not a priority. I have a different brief from the LEA for the next six months.'

Mr Hans was keen on Circle time:

> We did this a lot in my previous school, I have lots of information about it and it needs to be set up here. We had an INSET on PSHE from a person who has now left the school. Without someone at the helm it's not necessarily going anywhere.

He believed that assemblies needed to be more explicitly Christian and also include stories from other faiths too. 'At the moment they all 'do their own thing' and that's something that Ofsted pick up on.'

Mr Hans told me that recent Personal, Social and Health Education training for the staff had brought about a 'sea change'. He was hopeful that my research would be two way and that I would disseminate to staff techniques to encourage cultural awareness. He felt that this predominantly white school had 'a different set of problems to a multicultural school which was at an advantage in the first place because of the cultural exchange between pupils'.

At the end of my research in Exforth I brought in several PSHE and RE policies from other schools I had worked in, and gave staff booklists and information about multicultural resources to support the future development of multicultural education at the school. Mr Hans, then acting headteacher, seemed interested in issues of diversity but, unlike Deasham and Rarnlow schools' headteachers, he admitted that exploring diversity was not a priority. The newly appointed headteacher Mr Chalk gave a similar response: the school did not actively promote antiracism nor consider issues of diversity a priority.

Exforth junior school is located at the edge of a small town, surrounded by a mixture of detached and terraced housing. The modern buildings are set amidst an extensive playground and playing field area. There were 249 children on roll, 113 girls and 133 boys. From observation I estimated that 97 per cent of the pupils were white and 1 per cent of dual heritage Pakistani and white, and 2 per cent dual heritage African Caribbean and white.

An arson attack on Mrs Kelly's classroom was thought to have been started by a former pupil. All the children's work had been destroyed in the fire. Mrs Hart, the educational co-worker, told me it had really upset Mrs Kelly. She was a caring teacher but, like most of the teachers at the school, she used shouting and firm reprimands to maintain discipline. The children did not have the same friendly relationship with their teachers as was apparent in the other schools.

Relationships between staff and children – cultures of dominance
Exforth school was undergoing a period of change with several changes of headteacher and two long-term supply teachers. Unlike the other three schools it had an authoritarian ethos.

Whilst I was observing an art lesson, four boys talked to me about some of the teachers they liked, one of whom had brought in his baby to show them. They were talking in a fairly relaxed way to me but when their teacher Mr Penny came to look at their art work, they were very reticent. He told them: 'So long as you like what you're doing ... Hardly anyone claims to be any good ... like Maths it's good to enjoy it even if you're not good at it', thus implying that their work was not a very good, and revealing his low expectation of their work (Arthur *et al*, 2006).

A Year 3 teacher described the socio-economic background of the children in the following way:

> Some of the kids are from Manchester. Their families didn't pay their rates and so they moved them all here. X town is a real mix. For example once I did a sex education lesson with Year 5 and some of the kids knew everything. Whereas others – I felt really mean telling them, it would have been better if they'd have been left.

In a literacy lesson I observed, Mrs Lawton repeatedly shouted at the children to be quiet:

> How long do I have to wait! Caroline the longer I have to count up and down in 5's ... Lucas you can stop being so clever and counting backwards. There are some *very, very* rude children in this class who don't know when they're allowed to talk.

Even when other children were inattentive, Lucas (white) was always singled out. During another literacy lesson Mrs Lawton praised some of the children for their performance of 'Gran can you rap!' but some of the compliments were backhanded: 'Colin you've got a merit – your first one – you actually finished! Which is more than you did, Ruby. Colin actually finished, which is a bit of a change!'

Similarly at Registration one morning Mr Penny spoke severely to Toni (of Italian heritage) about being late. Toni displayed subdued and sub-missive body language as Mr Penny told him: 'Make sure you get here on time.' He asked the children to line up to go to Mrs Kelly's class for a video and sternly rebuked those who were not in line. The children stood still as Mr Penny passed. I felt that they were obedient out of fear of this tall, well-built man.

On another occasion Mandy told me about a residential visit to the Isle of Wight which had been organised for upper Key Stage 2 children but which had been cancelled, she said 'because there were loads of naughty children'.

Thus the ethos at Exforth school was one of authoritative teacher and subservient child (Jenkins, 1993; James, 1995), unlike the caring ethos which characterised Deasham and Rarnlow schools. However, the school was in a state of transition between headteachers and perhaps the teachers felt discipline had to be maintained in an authoritative way with their challenging pupils.

Lunchtimes and playtimes
Children were anxious to be allowed on to the field during breaktimes. They played on the playground until a teacher came out and blew a whistle, signalling permission to go on to the field. The field was dominated by boys playing football while the girls remained on the playground with the non-football-playing boys. During one playtime a football rolled to me; I kicked it and was ignored. It was as if non-football players did not exist. During my six weeks at the school I became

aware of the in set of footballers who constituted the gang. Two boys told me that: 'the gang tease us'.

When I asked why they were not members of the gang and whether any girls were, they replied: 'If they don't let us in, which they often don't, I don't think they'd let girls in.' The assumption was that this gang admitted only the fittest and most skilful male footballers. But some of the gang were more tolerant than others: 'I scored a goal once – Mark M lets me play but Dean doesn't. Dean hates me. If they are playing with Mark's football then Mark lets me play.'

One lunchtime the gang had no football and other forms of play emerged, which included playfighting, competitive running games and pushing games. In some schools contact or domination games are forbidden because of likely injuries. Many teachers feel that these games are masculine and that large areas which are dominated by boys playing these sorts of games marginalise the female or quiet activities. The culture of the gang boys dominated Exforth school, whereas children in Deasham were encouraged to use small play equipment and in Bently school running games and domination games were not allowed.

The children also told me about the school's anti-bullying strategy. Certain children wore anti- bullying mentor badges which signified that they could be approached when an incident occurred. Some of the children were cynical about this scheme as one of the anti-bullying mentors was known to be a bully. However one of the Year 6 bully mentors said, 'There was a bully who wrote [to apply to be a bully mentor], and got chosen, and he's not a bully anymore. It's snapped his brain out of bullying.'

Children at Exforth school were street-wise; they were more sophisticated than the others in how they dressed and in their attitudes towards the opposite sex. During one lunchtime a couple of children came to tell me that they 'fancied' someone. I noticed that few of the children wore school sweatshirts. Most wore jeans, shorts or skirts and T-shirts and some wore designer or fashion clothes. Lisette commented: 'There is a school uniform but no-one wears it'.

Cassie told me some of the rules about dress: 'You're not allowed jewellery in school. You can have plain sleepers [in your ears] if necessary. No shoulders or midriff bare.' Interestingly this type of rule was unnecessary in the other schools I visited as children did not seem inclined to wear such clothes.

One lunchtime I sat with two boys. As they did not speak I decided to remain silent too. The dining area was small, dark and airless. The dinner supervisors were strict about noise. Even a little noise in this small area might have been too loud but this meant that lunchtimes were not social occasions as in Rarnlow and Deasham. The main aim seemed to be to eat as quickly as possible and get outside to play.

Assemblies

The first assembly I attended at the school was also the first for Mr Hans, the interim headteacher. All the staff left the assembly, which, Mr Hans told me afterwards, he had not expected. The children were slow to settle and Mr Hans appealed to them: 'Show to me the courtesy I show to you.'

He told some traditional stories of the sun and the wind and the man and the donkey but left the children to work out the meanings. Throughout my time at Exforth I noticed several teachers, mostly supply teachers, raising their voices with the children; in contrast Mr Hans' style was quietly powerful and I could see why he liked the sun and wind story. The story tells how the calm but powerful sun can make a person take off their coat whereas the wild and raging wind fails to blow it away – the person buttons up their coat even tighter.

However the children seemed more used to being shouted at and as the assembly progressed I felt I should withdraw and let Mr Hans establish his relationship with the children without another adult observing him. Before I left I heard him say a prayer, 'Hands together eyes closed, Dear Lord, help us to be sensible'.)

Mr Hans was anxious to tell me later how uncomfortable he had felt about the assembly and said that in future all staff would be obliged to attend. The children were used to a culture of dominance and did not show respect towards someone who did not dominate.

Sport was a feature of many assemblies. One assembly, for example, began with a hymn practice of Christian hymns, followed by a lengthy discussion of the rugby tournament which Exforth school did not win. David, who was sitting by me, shouted: 'Because St C's [school] cheat.'

The theme of sport was continued by Mrs Kelly, who talked to the children about picking teams for rounders, reminding them that, 'When you're going out you're still part of this team'.

In an assembly taken by Mr Penny, the school was divided up and had a competition to see which side could sing the loudest. Mr Penny talked about 'sportsmanship'. He corrected himself once to say 'sportspersonship' but reverted to 'sportsmanship' for the rest of the assembly:

> This time of year it's good to get outside ... If you're not good at sport it doesn't matter. You can be good even if you are hopeless – it's how you play that matters – your attitude. Some adults give a bad example. It's up to the schools to put the balance right.

Mr Penny told a story about two famous sportsmen and concluded by saying that: 'Whoever wins it's important to give your opponent a clap. Next time if you lose, give them a clap. If you win give the losers a clap. Now give me a clap!' Mr Penny finished the assembly with a short prayer about making the best of all opportunities, followed by the Lord's prayer. A few days after this assembly, children in Mr Norris's class were discussing SATs during a literacy lesson and Mr Norris emphasised that these national tests were not the only indicators of success. He said, 'You might be a good sportsman, I mean sportsperson'. One child had obviously been listening to the assembly: 'That's what we did in assembly, the biggest cheaters always get found out!'

I observed an exceptional amount of sport at Exforth school in that hot summer term. A boy told me that 'often we have boys against girls, or sometimes in houses'.

The practice of pitting boys against girls has been abandoned in most schools. New thinking about gender equality means that grouping by gender is now discouraged (Moyles, 1995). Alison had told me: 'I'm a bit nervous about races because it's against boys'.

The children were interested in my notes and keen to tell me about themselves. I noticed that children rarely communicated with adults about their own lives but talked mainly about the task in hand or discipline issues.

Most days the children did games in the afternoon and I thought it odd that other curriculum subjects, such as RE, Music and Geography did not seem to be taught during the six weeks I was there. However the visit was towards the end of the summer term and it was warm, so I guessed that staff decided to abandon these subjects in favour of games outside. When I asked staff, they said that RE had been timetabled the previous half-term. Mrs Kelly admitted that, 'No one is specifically in charge of RE. There was someone who was ill and then went to another school.' Mr Hans confided that 'There is no RE co ordinator – well there was a fundamentalist but I felt that would be inappropriate'. When I asked the children, they said they could not remember doing any RE since the Autumn term or even the previous year.

> Mandy: Instead of music we do circle time.
>
> Sarah: There is orchestra on Friday afternoons. [This only involved the children who played an instrument.]
>
> Ben: We don't do Geography no more. We do have hymn practice.
>
> [Another child showed her timetable]
>
> Simon: We do RE sometimes.
>
> James: We did God and stuff, the Jews, different religions, the Jewish religion. But we did it so long ago I've forgotten. We haven't got new RE books, they got burnt in the fire. We looked at certain beliefs – one was the Buddha.

Stuart summed up the criteria for the occurrence of RE: 'We don't do RE if it's sunny – we do PE outside. In RE we watch a video of Islam, Buddha, allsorts. We watch the video and write down what we've watched.'

> Martha: What's Buddha?
>
> Stuart: He wasn't a king, he was ... a prince at one time, he meditated people. We go into Mrs Kelly's room. We do RE with the opposite teacher and swap RE and PE.

Mrs Kelly took most of the RE lessons while Mr Penny took the PE, but if it was sunny, everyone went outside for games.

I asked another group of children about the provision of RE in the school.

> Mike: RE we don't really do it much now.

Kevin: God is dead now. It's really crazy but we don't do it much now, not sure why, it just stopped suddenly. We did loads nearly every day.

Mike: When did we do loads?

Kevin: 'Until this year started, we did about religions, Buddha and stuff.'

Louise: We learn about other religions, celebrations and how they live. We've not done it for a while, we've not watched any videos.

In another group, Lara commented,

RE stands for Religious Exercises. It's really boring. We watch videos and write stuff off sheets filling in the missing word about Pharaohs like Buddha.

Kim corrected her: 'Not Pharaohs – that's history. We did symbols in religions, like the cross and the circle with dots in ying yang. I don't know ... I think it means peace. I know a lot about what we dream about.' Silas added: 'She's not human, they probed her – she's an alien.'

To acknowledge any interest in dreams or religious symbols was clearly unusual and 'not normal' for Silas. I felt that this summed up the parochial climate at Exforth school. There seemed to be an ethos of the acceptable 'normal' characterised by white western privilege and bourgeois attitudes and the unacceptable 'unusual' characterised by the spiritual, ethnic minority and alternative lifestyle.

During a quiet reading session Mrs Kelly played a tape by the Eurythmics which, the children said, was unusual during lesson times except in art lessons. The atmosphere was relaxed and the children obviously enjoyed the reading session, sitting comfortably engaged in their books. On the wall were wax pastel pictures of Aboriginal Dreamtime. The children told me that Mrs Kelly gave out some postcards with Aboriginal dreamtime scenes, which they used as an inspiration to draw their own. They could not remember having a discussion about these Aboriginal pictures and no one could tell me about the spiritual context of dreamtime. Maybe they had forgotten. A few pockets of good practice were in evidence concerning RE and spiritual development.

Mr Norris, a supply teacher for the term, had this to say about imperial and metric measurements in a maths lesson:

We think of America as being dead modern but in fact it uses this ancient imperial measurement of 12 inches make a foot, a dozen and so on ... Whereas we use metric which is easier. It's to do with where we live ... We invented miles but because we're near Europe, Italy and France, we use metric. Americans aren't European. They don't use kilograms, they use tonnes – which is old fashioned.

Mr Norris was challenging the stereotype of the superiority of American culture. But there was no discussion: He just gave his polemic. A group from his class told me: 'We did Islamic patterns in Maths with Mr Norris.'

Mr Norris seemed aware of different cultures and endeavoured to present diversity in his teaching. He seemed willing to raise controversial issues. His literacy lesson involved the children discussing vivisection and the advantages of using animals to find cures for serious illnesses. He asked them: 'You don't need make-up and perfume but if your parents were dying, would you use a treatment tested on animals?'

At the end of the first phase of the research I collected together Exforth school policies and other information from the Personal Social and Health Education in-service training sessions. These pointed to good practice in principle but there was little sign that any of it was implemented. Each policy itemised the responsibilities for the co-ordinator, how the subject related to other subjects, planning, resources, equal opportunities, assessment and effectiveness indicators. The Music and History policies mentioned other cultures, for example in the equal opportunities section for Music:

> Music is taught to all children regardless of their ability, gender, race or cultural background. Stereotypical views are challenged and we encourage pupils to appreciate and view positively differences in others. The programme of study includes themes and subjects based on the music of non-western cultures.

Significantly, there was no RE policy. In Year 5 RE was timetabled for 25 minutes on a Friday afternoon between games and assembly but I did not observe any RE lesson taking place. I did observe numerous games lessons.

Bently school – Predominantly White, City Location

The research at Bently school, the fourth school in the study, was undertaken after 9/11. During my first visit, six months earlier, Mrs Kite, the headteacher, was enthusiastic about taking part in the research. She was personally interested in cultural diversity and drew my attention to the local LA manual *Managing Cultural Diversity* (Derby City Council, 2000). She had attended a course run by the LA advisor for RE and Citizenship based on this manual. She told me that a few years earlier:

> The juniors failed their Ofsted. It was a difficult time. I was asked to be head of the Juniors and the infants – the schools amalgamated. It was a difficult time. But now we are moving forward. There was anxiety but we're getting there.

Bently school is located in the middle of a 1930s housing estate in a rather poor part of the city. The local community is predominantly white. The school building is Victorian, spacious and well maintained. There is a relatively small playground for the junior children. A nearby field is available for sports activities but not for playing on at breaktime and lunchtime.

As I walked around the school I noticed various multicultural displays. Year 1's display about the festival Divali had 'Happy Divali' written in English, Punjabi, Bengali and Hindi. There were *mendhi* patterns which children had completed in sewing lessons. A book display in the hall included *Amazing Grace* (Hoffman and Binch, 1994) in English and Urdu. There was also the Big book *A is for Africa* (Onyefulu, 1999). Each presents positive views of the diversity of life in some African countries.

There were 294 children in the infants and juniors combined. The 61 Year 5 children were organised into three classes, one taken by Mrs Pink, one taken by Mrs Reade and a mixed Year 5 and 6 class taken by Mrs Port. I was told that of the 294 children, 143 received free school meals, indicating that many were from low socio-economic backgrounds. About 5 per cent of children came from an ethnic minority background, British Asian, and dual heritage African Caribbean and white.

A new and enthusiastic RE coordinator had been appointed. She showed me a scheme of work she had produced and notes for teachers to support the teaching and learning. She was a reception teacher and the notes were comprehensive for the Foundation stage and the Infants and firmly anchored in the local agreed syllabus. But the Junior RE programme just had a series of questions taken from the QCA material, which is non-statutory, such as 'Where did the Christian Bible come from?' and 'Why is Muhammed important to Muslims?' (QCA, 2000).

Another teacher had worked on a citizenship programme eleven years ago and was keen to discuss the children's awareness of diversity and racism. She and her partner had been involved in the Racism part of the programme and her partner was still involved. But she had not communicated her experience to other members of staff and lamented the fact that 'Not many people are interested in this type of stuff'.

Relationships between staff and children

Many teachers at Bently had positive and egalitarian relationships with children. There were a few teachers who dominated the children and it was interesting to notice the different ways in which one child, Bart, behaved with teachers who used differing management styles.

Bart displayed challenging behaviour in many lessons. Mrs Pink treated him firmly but kindly and he usually settled down to work after any outburst. Bart's mother worked as a helper in school and as she passed by he always gave her a hug and a kiss, showing no embarrassment. But this same child acted very differently in Mr Benn's literacy class for less able children. As soon as the lesson began, he spoke to Bart and Louise:

> Mr Benn: Louise get your book and do it [the work] unless you want a cross by your name. Bart your name goes on the board.
>
> Bart: But Mr Benn I wasn't even talking.

During a spelling test Bart asked to go to the toilet and Mr Benn refused. Bart's body language was completely different from what I had observed in lessons with Mrs Pink, where he had been relaxed and happy. Here he sulked and buried his head in his hands and said, 'But I have a letter'. He got out of his seat and went anyway. Mr Benn gave me a look to say, 'See what I have to deal with'. I felt that he did not get the best out of the children and did not contribute to the caring ethos of the school.

Mrs Pink had a very different behaviour management style. She had negotiated some classroom rules with her class of 26 Year 5 children. The school was trialling an 'assertive discipline' strategy (Canter, 1992) which involved the children being rewarded for 'good' behaviour. A 'good' act or mark was rewarded by a child colouring in a wizard picture on a display board. The display board told children:

> When our Wizard is filled in our treat will be – extra time in the computer suite. Wizard thinks these should be our classroom rules:

- Follow all rules to get the best marks and most fun
- Always put your hand up to answer a question
- Be friendly and considerate to each other
- Always listen to what adults are saying
- Respect school's and other people's property

A School Council had been set up and two children were chosen to represent each class. I chatted about it to Louise, Matthew and Ryan, all British white. Louise told me that the children in Mrs Pink's class negotiated issues with her: 'Some of us wanted to put up a display and Mrs Pink said – 'It's your classroom you can do what you want'. So we [representatives on the school council] put up a display about the school council.'

Mrs Reade exemplified Bently school's caring ethos when she abandoned a history lesson one afternoon and instead discussed behaviour problems during a circle time. She began by saying:

> Mrs Read: I'm spending a lot of time sorting out problems – children falling out with each other and not telling an adult. You can rely on each other. What if Sally was upset by Simon – then Belinda could be told. What is Belinda's role? You can share things with a friend. What are the barriers which stop you from telling an adult?
>
> Kurt: Name calling! If you tell an adult people call you a tell-tale.
>
> Mrs Reade: There was once a girl who was bullied, but once adults knew the problem it was sorted. The worry goes away. The bully only has power while you keep it a secret. You always need to tell someone – an adult or a friend. A problem shared is a problem halved.

The children were finding solutions to their problems with support from a teacher who did not act in an authoritative way like staff in Exforth school and Mr Benn in Bently. Rather, they negotiated with and worked alongside children to address issues of power. There was a climate of encouragement and rewards for good work and behaviour rather than derision and punishment for bad behaviour and poor work. During a literacy lesson Mrs Pink gave out stickers to those who tried hard and gave good answers.

After one disastrous lunchtime for Nick, Mrs Pink tried to turn the situation around. She put her arm around Nick and said to the watching children 'Nick is finding playtimes difficult. He wants someone to be his playtime partner.' Kay and Liam offered, and Mrs Pink replied 'Thank you children. This will help keep you [Nick] out of trouble. Keeping you away from people.' The children commented that when you get angry it's hard. So Nick's playtime partners were to cheer him up and try to calm him down. This was a special moment between Mrs Pink and her class. Everyone showed genuine care for Nick and Nick's smile of relief, appreciation and feeling of belonging was in marked contrast to his earlier look of aggression.

Mrs Reade's characteristic egalitarian attitude was challenged by a new boy, Jonathon, who started in Mrs Reade's class. He was French speaking, had lived in France and was of African heritage. He had spent time in the Congo before moving to Paris. Mrs Reade seemed very perturbed. She saw Jonathon as a 'problem' and his language as a barrier rather than a resource.

> Mrs Reade: It's a learning curve for us. He's fluent in French. My French isn't very good. I've got him sitting next to Charles – he's a good influence. There's a boy in Mrs Pink's class who's not a good influence. The other children wanted to come and see him. I said 'no, just our class at the moment'. He comes right out in French and asks for things – he's very confident. I'm absolutely tired from translating. The Head speaks good French.

I found that Jonathon was regarded as a novelty, possibly because he spoke French but also because he was black. When I asked Mark if the boy was new he answered:

> What, the coloured one? Yes he's new.

During a literacy lesson where Mrs Pink and the children discussed some spellings, I felt happy and relaxed like the children. Mrs Pink remarked to me:

> Yes, we have a good relationship with the children. But it wasn't always so. The school was in special measures. I think it was due to an ineffective head who went off on sick leave and was always having days out. Mrs Kite has turned it around. The staff are the same, it's just she's a strong head. Three years ago I had nine behavioural problem children – I was on the verge of a nervous breakdown.

I observed a School Council session where the children were given the opportunity to discuss such issues as the too small furniture in Mrs Pink's class, and bullying and playtime partners.

Lunchtimes and playtimes

The children were well aware of the specified zones in the playground: the talking zone, the bat and ball zone and the skipping zone. They were not allowed to run as the playground area was too small. I could see the frustration in the faces of some of the children, who obviously needed an outlet for their energy. Yet there were relatively few incidents of bad behaviour because the zone system was understood and the whole area was effectively supervised. Any child who misbehaved on the playground was sent to another teacher's class after break and not allowed to work with their own group: this punishment effectively discouraged such incidents. (This contrasts with the aggressive ethos of Exforth's playtime.)

The children had to line up in the 'assembly line' every time they moved around the school from outside play to the classroom; from the classroom to the dining hall; from one room to another. The line was organised by the teacher, who split up noisy, lively or potentially badly behaved individuals, ensuring that misbehaviour was kept to a minimum. It seemed to work.

I chatted quietly as I went with the children to lunch. There was a positive atmosphere in the dining room and the children sat in groups. Talking was allowed and the seating area was large, well-ventilated and bright. As at Deasham and Rarnlow schools, lunchtimes were a social event and the children chatted happily.

During a wet playtime break the dinner supervisor left Mrs Pink's class playing a hand game and the children gained a wizard point for behaving well in her absence.

Assemblies

One assembly I observed began with a Christian song 'We are climbing Jacob's ladder' and all the infants and some of the lower juniors did the actions accompanying the lyrics. Friday assembly was totally given over to awards and certificates. Each teacher described why they had chosen a particular child to be 'Star of the Week':

Mrs Hope: Mary for her work in gymnastics

Mr Ridly: John for consistent hard work and for being well- mannered.

Mrs Reade: The whole of class 16 for helping Jonathon settle in.

While obviously well-meaning, this singled Jonathon out as being more difficult to settle in than a white child with fluent English. Thus Jonathon was portrayed as a problem that class 16 and presumably Mrs Reade herself managed to settle in well under difficult circumstances. I am sure it was intended to be an honour for the whole class, but it created a negative perception of the ethnic minority child. Jonathon was the only person in the class not to receive the award and was left sitting, looking confused, while the rest of his class was presented with the award.

Curriculum issues

Mrs Reade invited children to answer the register in different languages, to promote a variety of cultures. Mrs Pink named her Literacy groups after characters from books – all of them white males: James (and the Giant Peach), BFG (big friendly giant), Charlie (and the Chocolate Factory) and Danny (Champion of the World).

When discussing different subjects, few children mentioned RE. Eventually Michelle said 'Oh and RE. We looked at the Bible and picked stories out.'

I was able to observe one RE lesson with Mrs Pink's class. She set the tone with her opening comment: 'The quicker we can get the RE done the quicker we can get to the ICT suite.'

The children had been looking at the Christian Bible and knew about the different types of literature in it – as Alison explained, 'stories, advice wisdom, poetry, prayer'.

The children had RE books which doubled up as topic books at the back. There were enough Children's Bibles for the children to share one between two. The children thought carefully about some of the stories. When discussing the martyrdom of Steven in the Acts of the Apostles, Bart and Louise asked, 'What does it mean – he died for his faith? What does faith mean?' The children discussed this together and deduced that Steven had died for what he believed in. Bart said, 'They shouldn't be harmed for believing in Jesus. It should be like it is nowadays. But they are probably harmed in Australia, Germany and Africa.'

The children were asked for a summary of their story at the end of the lesson. They had attempted to engage with the stories so there was some evidence of learning about religion – but there was no clear learning from religion (QCA, 2004). Mrs Pink did not discuss the authority of the Bible for some Christians or compare it with authority sources in the children's lives. Neither did she discuss the meaning of the stories for Christian believers, or how the stories had affected the children's attitudes towards a particular issue. The discussion revolved around the content, for example, Mrs Pink commented: 'the ten Laws are not stories but Instructions. The prayer of Jesus – what do we call it? Do we still say it now? It's been altered slightly, well, not altered but rather it's just a different translation.'

Here Mrs Pink was identifying herself and the children with Christianity by saying 'we'. Thus Christianity was the norm and other religious beliefs were what 'the other' people have. In a later discussion with the children this was confirmed: 'Indians, Muslims, like go to the mosque like we go to church' said John.

Jeremy explained the RE he was doing in Mrs Port's class:

> I'm in a mixed class so I do different RE. RE is all different religions like Hinduism. It's religion when people celebrate Divali – like we celebrate Christmas. They celebrate Divali and the English people celebrate Christmas. Divali – it's a time of light. They mostly read the story of Rama and Sita.

Sam gave a comprehensive account of the Rama and Sita story. He concluded by saying: 'I don't know if it's true. They like that story, like we believe in Jesus and God.'

Claire told me:

> We talked about the Bible and Mrs Reade said that it's the best selling book because it tells you, all around the world, what things happened in the Old Testament. In Religious Education you learn about Jesus and other religions. There are different kinds of texts in Jesus' times [texts] in all old words. Muslims they believe in Adam and Eve.

During a science lesson the children in Mrs Reade's group were discussing absorption of sound. Mrs Reade grew frustrated at not being able to translate the lesson to Jonathon, the French-speaking new boy of African heritage. There was no attempt to demonstrate and allow him to play with the materials. Rather, Mrs Reade wanted to 'instruct' Jonathon so that he would have the same 'knowledge' as the rest of the class.

I observed a Geography lesson about France in Mrs Port's class. The children 'thought showered' what they knew already, some of which was stereotypical:

> French accents
> Disneyland
> They drive on the opposite side of the road
> The Eiffel Tower
> They eat frogs' legs
> The capital is Paris
> They eat croissants
> They eat snails, scorpions and worms.

There was no thought of asking Jonathon to visit the class and talk about France – possibly with a parent – which seemed to me to be a missed opportunity. The children looked in books and were set the task of making an information sheet about France.

I believe the caring ethos of Bently school was influential for Max and Bart. Both boys displayed an understanding of antiracism. Yet they also displayed negative views and these seemed to be due to the negative relationship they had with Mr Benn. Their immaturity and low ability may also have been factors. None of the children, apart from Daljit, had a comprehensive knowledge of the variety of religions represented in the UK and their RE was limited.

4
Being British and cultural identity

I'm orange (Kurt, Exforth School)

This chapter considers

- the concepts of identity and culture
- children's attitudes towards being British concerning skin colour, being born and living in Britain and speaking English
- choosing their own identity, dual cultures and religions and remaining in their own culture.

The concept of culture is explored with reference to ethnic minority groups, Islam and the media, popular culture and post-modernism.

Identity and culture

The concepts of identity and culture overlap. Culture can only be understood in terms of how people identify themselves as being part of and makers of a particular culture (Modood *et al*, 1997). This use of the word culture came to be adopted by the children in my research. It was they who decided how we should go about answering my research question – 'What is your knowledge and attitude towards your own and other people's cultures?' We talked about what was meant by the word culture and they suggested the following list, which we used as an *aide memoire* on the bean prompt sheets (see appendix Table 1) filled in by the children prior to the interview:

- What food they eat
- What they wear

- What they do
- What they look like
- What they believe

In their study of ethnic minority groups, Modood *et al* (1997) had a similar list, but without food. Modood notes (p291) that there is a 'new form of ethnic identity emerging which supercedes former ideas' about the concept of culture.

There is no entity out there called culture which I could define here. Culture is socially constructed, so throughout this section my definitions refer not to a real entity but a construction. To inform this discussion I draw on the perceptions of culture presented by scholars. Strinati (1995), Storrey (1996), Hall (1996) and Delanty and Strydom (2003). Together with 'culture' I include the concept of identity, particularly that of cultural identity. Culture has been defined as high art or popular (mass) culture, to do with aesthetics and with being human. The social construction of what it constitutes may also have a political or some other agenda (Storrey, 1996).

British identity was considered in the Parekh Report *The Commission on the Future of Multi-Ethnic Britain* (2000). It considered the complex nature of British society and how peopled might live in a 'community of communities' maintaining their identity without jeopardising social cohesion.

Being British equals being white

There has been much discussion recently about immigration and British identity, especially at election and by-election times. There is a Britishness test, *Life in the UK* (Border and Immigration Agency, 2007), and the Home Secretary apparently resigned in 2007 because of his department's mismanagement of the release of immigrants found guilty of crimes and due to be deported. Children listen to the news and their parents' and others' opinions about news items and begin to formulate ideas from an early age about being British and who is 'in' and 'not in' the British club. Brown (1998) points out that prejudice is not innate but learned.

Most of the children in my research deemed British identity to be dependent on being born in Britain, being white, having British parents, and speaking English. This finding is similar to that of Carrington and Short (1998). Children often had a change of mind after initially disagreeing with the proposal that a Hindu family in a picture I showed them could be British. After reflection, many of the children said they could be British Asians if they were born here, or if they spoke English. Some of the low socio-economic and some of the less able British white children in my study considered British whites the only category of 'true' Britishness.

The following extract exemplifies this attitudes towards being British. Liam, James and Nicola, three white children from Bently school, which is predominantly white, discuss whether the people from the pictures were British:

Sally: Are all the people in these pictures, are they all British?

James: Yeah.

Nicola: No! Not all of them

Sally: Which are and which aren't ?

Nicola: This isn't [picture of British Hindu family]. It doesn't look like it

Sally: What would you need to look like to be British?

Nicola: Well they wear different clothes and they're eating different food

Sally: So to be British you have to wear certain clothes and eat certain food?

James: Miss some British eat their [own] food and sometimes wear their clothes if one of our religions marry another religion, then sometimes they choose to wear their religion's one

Nicola: If they like wear turbans on their head, we only wear like caps and hats. If it's winter we wear like woolly hats

Sally: And are they British, James? What would you have to look like to be British ?

James: Something like this picture, [white people in Buddhist posture] Picture H describes it. Some people believe in other religions

Sally: Right so you think [picture] H shows people believing in another religion? How do you know that?

James: Cos like when like ... For example Pakistani, we go to church they go to mosque. That looks like a mosque – I've seen it on the telly.

Many children in my schools found it difficult to identify exactly what British white was. This is not easy, as there are myriad strains of white such as British Polish, Geordie, Northern Irish, Greek and white Jews (Nayak, 1999). It is important for British whites to examine their own ethnicity – although Sheets (2000) fears that some authors who write about the diversity of white culture are merely ensuring that white culture is given centre stage again (Dilig, 1999; Howard, 1999, 2000; MacIntyre, 1997).

Being British – skin colour

Children spoke about skin colour. Just as the word black is used as an umbrella term for Asian, Caribbean, African and so on, so white can be a term which covers a large number of discrete ethnic and cultural groups. The white Western privilege discussed here relates to the white American or English culture which is promoted in the media (Hafez, 2000). This monocultural view of Britain is challenged by scholars (eg. Modood *et al*, 1997; Modood *et al*, 2006). Most children in the predominantly white schools believed the 'in' club of Britishness was restricted to white, Christian people and they had little awareness of the diversity within whiteness. Neither did they have an appreciation of ethnic minority groups such as Asian, African Caribbean and Chinese heritage being British.

During an interview in Bently school, a white girl, Fiona, Claire of African/white heritage and Daljit, British Asian Sikh, discussed Britishness. Claire and Fiona argued that a British person was someone who is white, Christian and able to speak English, yet they also accepted that their friend Daljit was British, even though her skin was not white and she was Sikh. This is similar to Troyna and Hatcher's (1992) findings, where children make exceptions for their friends, who may not be part of the 'in' group but are nevertheless accepted:

> Fiona: I wouldn't describe the people from all different cultures as being British because they probably speak a different language and have a different coloured skin and I think sometimes ... it could be different to what British people do
>
> Sally: So to be British, what colour skin do you [have]?
>
> Fiona: It's like peachy colour but the other it's either a really dark brown or a light brown like Daljit's.

Sally: Right – so would you say Daljit is British then?

Fiona: Yeah yeah – I would say she's British because she can speak our language

Sally: So you have to speak what language to be British?

Fiona: English, I'll say English because if eemmm you're English and someone speaks a different language to you you won't understand them so I don't think they're kind of British

Claire: I think that 'no'. I don't think everyone is British because they won't have different cultures, they will believe in Christianity not Sikh or any others – I think they would talk eat look dress and write the same as us ....

Fiona: On picture L [of a white family] this is what I think – people are British. Because I think that if they're British that's what people will look like. If they're not British, they probably wouldn't have all that stuff in the garden, or they probably wouldn't be a peachy coloured skin.

The next extract from Bently school is interesting in the way the children talked about the literal colours of people's skins. Bart and Michelle are white, Kurt is dual heritage Caribbean and white:

Bart: Because I don't know a lot about British white ... because British white – you don't see many of them around but if you do, you don't know they are British white sometimes. ...

Sally: Right so who would you describe as British white people – are there British white people in this school?

Michelle: Loads of them

Kurt: Yeah all the teachers are

Michelle: All the kids are

Kurt: I'm orange

Sally: What did you say?

Kurt: I'm orange

Sally: You're orange?

Bart: Looks like brown

Kurt: I'm half caste

Michelle: And Shanice is

Sally: What do you mean by half caste Kurt?

Kurt: Cos my mum – I think she's from Jamaican and errm and so that makes me half caste but I don't know what half caste means

Sally: Ok and what's your Dad? ...

Kurt: ... he's not from Jamaica – he's half he's quarter German

A black colleague told me that so often black children in white societies feel they have to name the colour of their outward appearance to show they have pigeonholed themselves in the pecking order. In this instance Kurt did not conform. Perhaps he was creating his own identity (see Chapter 5).

Following a discussion about a picture of a Hindu family, I asked three British Asian girls 'How can you tell from the skin colour whether they're British?'

Francesca: If you're born near the equator you have probably dark skin cos of the atmosphere, if you're born in England then you would have lighter skin because it's not as hot as near the equator.

Sally: So you're saying that they've got lighter skin than in B [picture of Hindu family]?

Emma: Yes maybe the grandma is Indian maybe those two are from the top part of India. This one may not be fully British might be actually born in Africa ...

Francesca: Yes some British white people are actually Asian – its just their skin colour's been really light. Like I know someone, my friend, my mum's friend umm I think it's sister, she's really light and I think she's a Christian but she's Asian

Sally: Is that right?

Monica: Everyone thinks that my brother isn't Indian and they say he's Italian – he's really fair and he's got that hint of brown in it so he looks Italian. [Giggling] But he's Asian but they think he's Italian

So here the children appreciate that the literal colour of a person's skin is not a reliable indicator for determining a person's heritage.

Being British – living in Britain, speaking English
The three girls from Deasham school discussed being British. Melissa is British Caribbean and Christian, Zoe and Kate are British Asian and Muslim:

Zoe: It says on this sheet that 'would you describe people from all these cultures, all these different cultures, as British?' And I've said 'yes I would', because they're living in England they, obviously become British

Melissa: Not really, I've put 'not really' because it says 'would you describe the people from all these cultures as British?' No, cos I'm not being nasty, but some of them don't talk proper British they talk their own language ... No I wouldn't describe them as British – well they are British but they do not talk how British, like how British people should really talk. Some of my friends don't talk right they say 'It be's tomorrow'. Somehow they talk like that ...This is a proper English family [a picture of a white family] – she's got blue hair!

Thus Melissa assumed that 'proper British' people are white, like the family in this picture. This perception is echoed in the next extract.

Two boys from Deasham, Roy and Carlo who are Muslim and Jason, dual heritage African /white, suggested that people can choose whether or not to call themselves British. Both Carlo and Roy made derogatory remarks about Pakistan at the end of the discussion and declared that they preferred living in Britain.

Carlo: No [people in the pictures of Sikhs, Muslims and Hindus of Asian heritage] because they came from a different place

Sally: What if they came from a different place and then lived here?

Carlo: They are British

Kirsten: Then you wouldn't call them British because they come from a different place. These [indicates pictures of white people] are British.

Sally: So are all the other people not British?

Jason: They can call themselves British if they want to, but if they don't want to, they don't have to

Sally: You all said earlier that you'd describe yourselves as British.

Roy: Yes Miss because I've lived here all my life

Carlo: Miss if you come from another country and stay here for the rest of my life, then I'd call myself British but I might go back to Pakistan. But I'd rather stay here than go back to Pakistan

Sally: Why?

Carlo: Because it's not a good place Miss. The roads aren't properly made. The cars and the vans and buses, they be packed of people, and you have to stand up and sometimes you fall down because of the bumps on the road

> Roy: And Miss if you have an accident and go to hospital they charge you money for the operations
>
> Carlo: They take the money first and if they can't save the person they still take the money.

Some children from Rarnlow school said that British identity was determined by whether one lives in Britain, and that people who are here on holiday do not fall within this category. Similarly if parents were on holiday in another country when the child was born, the child would still be British. Asian heritage children discussed British identity, and they too consider the place of birth to be significant. Francesca, British Asian and Hindu, chose a western pseudonym, as did Monica, who is British Asian and Sikh. Emma was of Malysian heritage:

> Monica: Because some might have come from like all around the world and they've just come to live here and they're not fully British
>
> Sally: So to be fully British you are saying you have to be born here?
>
> All: Not really
>
> Monica: Like you could have like a mother from Derby or ... but she's an Indian as well or Jamaican or something and ...
>
> Emma: You could have like the mother of the child born in somewhere, like India, and the child was born in like England – but they are still British
>
> Sally: Uh huh. But what about the mother who was from India?
>
> Emma: She'll be partly British and partly Indian, their child would be ...
>
> Sally: British?
>
> Emma: Yeah
>
> Sally: So how would you describe yourselves?
>
> Monica: I think I'm British because I was born in Britain

In an interview in Exforth school the three British white girls referred to the immigration issue, which had been recent headline news, when they discussed British identity:

> Liz: there's been in the news about people escaping into Britain and they've been taken back because they're not allowed in and stuff
>
> Louisa: ... they have actually come here and like they are British
>
> Faye: I put they are a different culture

Louisa: They are a different culture but if they've been here quite a long time then I'd call them British.

The following exchange at Rarnlow school between myself and Manpreet demonstrated this point. I also asked the children to consider the concept of British identity on a personal level, Carrington and Short (1998) asked questions in more abstract terms. I tried to find out what children thought by asking them about their own, their parents' and their friends' identities, thus making the situations more concrete.

Sally: Is it the word 'British' that you are not sure about? When I say 'British Asian' is it that that you think they might not be British?

Manpreet: When you say British Asian I think you mean the people that are Asian but they live in Britain ... My mum she was born in India but she came down here to umm get married, and then well she lived here for ever now, but we went to India the few past weeks – I can't remember ...

Sally: So would you mind me asking would you say your mum is British?

Manpreet: I don't know, cos she was born in India

Sally: She lives here now and will do for the rest of her life, apart from visiting?

Manpreet: I don't know, she might move, we might move to India or something like that

Sally: but while she's living in this country and thinking that she's ...

Manpreet: I think she would yeah

Sally: would you say that she's British, would she describe herself as British?

Manpreet: I don't know

Sally: Do you describe her as British?

Manpreet: Yeah because she lives in Britain ... Actually I think I'll say she really isn't Britain because she was raised in India and she'd probably not be a Britain.

It is significant that the Home Office UK passport service is clear on the issue of who is eligible for British passports – and who is therefore a British national:

As a foreign national or Commonwealth citizen you may have been granted the right to stay in the UK for an unlimited time, but this does not give you British nationality or make you eligible for a British passport. (British Passports, 2006)

Anyone who is a British citizen is entitled to apply for a British passport. This includes people who were born in the United Kingdom, in a British colony and had the right of abode in the UK, have been naturalised in the United Kingdom, have registered as a citizen of the United Kingdom and Colonies or who could prove legitimate descent from a father to whom one of the above conditions applied. Before the introduction of the British Nationality Act 1981, a person could not claim nationality from his or her mother. Those born in a British colony who had no right of abode in the UK will not become British citizens. British passports can be applied for by British Nationals (British Passports, 2006).

Being British – born in Britain

The issue of British identity was also discussed with reference to being born in Britain. Lucy, of Asian heritage, mentioned British passports. Other issues were raised by Maxwell, a white boy:

> Lucy: People who are born here I put, are [British]. [pause] and they have British passports

> Maxwell: Because people call them Chinese and so they're not British are they? Cos if they come to this country they're not British they're still Chinese [pause] I think ... so if someone came from like Germany into this country they'd still be German.

> Sally: Right but what about the people in these pictures here, are they British?

> Maxwell: Perhaps [pause] I think I got that one wrong

> Sally: No whatever you think is absolutely fine

> Maxwell: Cos I thought like, what do you describe, no, yeah, the people from all these different cultures as British ... People like come to this country and they're still like [pause] like Lucy, she came to this country, and she's still Indian

> Lucy: No! I was born here, my dad's mum was from India

> Sally: Ok so would you describe yourself as British then Lucy?

> Lucy: No cos my family like, you know, my dad's mum is from India, so yeah, we probably are, cos my Dad was born in India ...

> Maxwell: If you want to be British you have to be born in this country.

The children went on to discuss how people 'act' British. They were not alluding to British white here. They also talked about how people speak

70

with different accents: they concluded by together defining their different identities. They got on well together, although they did not play together or sit together in lessons. All three gave considered opinions on issues of racial identity: Daniel, of dual heritage Black African and British white, Lucy of Asian heritage and Maxwell, white said:

Daniel: ... like my mum she's umm she was born in Uganda and she came and lived here and she doesn't sound Ugandan here, she doesn't have that accent anymore ... English, I think I'm English

Lucy: African English

Daniel: African yeah. I just call myself English African, because I was born here

Sally: Cos that relates to what we were saying earlier [about Lucy] doesn't it? That's what I'm interested in finding out

Daniel: She's sort of English Indian

Lucy: Yeah cos I was born in India

Maxwell: You look like me when I'm tanned, when I've really got tanned

Below, three white girls in Exforth school consider the concept of British identity. They use assimilation language (Figueroa, 1995) to describe how Asian people might want to 'blend in':

Lisette: They might wear their own clothes or they might wear ours – it depends – it's their choice really ...

Violet: Well ... Asian people, who ... or whatever, who are coming to our country on holiday or something and they just might want to blend in with our kind of clothes. They might buy some of our clothes and take them back and show them, the other people in their country, and those people might come to our country and try and get some of our clothes so like they want to blend in with us

Sally: But what about the Asian people that came to this country a long long time ago and their children were born in this country

Lisette: Well you might have your mum or dad might say to you one day, right we're going on holiday next week to where we used to live. But you don't know about it because you were born in this country so it'd be nice for them to go and see what clothes they wear there

Two white boys from Exforth school, Spike and Toni, discussed Toni's nationality. He was of Italian heritage. They considered being brown as both a racist term and also that it signifies being tanned by the sun.

Jamie-Lee, a white girl, stated that if people came to live in Britain then their children would be British. 'Britishness' was highlighted by a white boy also from Exforth school:

> Mark: Yes I would [say everyone we've spoken about is British], because they do everything like British people. But then they've got a different religion, so they worship a different religion than British people; but they do jobs like British people – paper rounds like a lot of British kids do; and grown ups, like if they're a solicitor or something; that's what I've put.

In the research the children provided a wide range of views about British identity and related this to the concept of culture. I assumed the role of 'traveller' rather than 'miner' (Erricker, 2001) – I listened to what the children told me rather than having a particular theory to be proved or disproved. Categories sprang from the data and children's responses were grouped (see appendix for my research methods).

Cultural identity

The concept of identity permeated the children's discussions about culture. They had decided to include the questions 'Are cultures separate/ Does everyone have a culture?', in the Rarnlow school version of the Bean Sheet (Table 1 in the appendix), because Terri, a white girl from this multi-ethnic school had asked about this during one of the first focus groups. Terri's focus group discussed the complexity of culture, for example that some people were of dual heritage. Some children felt that culture and religion were closely linked and asked whether, if people did not subscribe to a particular religion, it meant that they had no culture? During the focus groups I tried not to influence the discussion and did not contribute answers to the questions.

Choosing your identity

Some children talked about choosing their own identity, as opposed to being born into a particular culture with a particular identity. British white was categorised as normal by some children from Bently school. Joseph and Louise, both British white, discussed culture:

> Louise: ... people have a right to choose their own culture.
>
> Joseph: What do you mean by that because when someone is born they've got their own culture – it's not up to them to choose a different culture, they'll be still speaking a culture ... Like what are you? Half Irish or somat?

Louise: I'm normal

Joseph: You're just normal English? Like if you were born in America and you wanted, and you were English, you were born as an English person, and you came over to this country and you wanted to change, go back to America and be American, you'd still be English even in America so you can't choose your own culture

Sally: Do you think you can?

Louise: You can yeah

Joseph: You can't. If you've got like American

Louise: You can

Joseph: And you want to be English how you going to be English?......

Sally: And can you choose your religion?

Joseph: No. My dad says you can never choose your own culture or religion

Louise: That's your dad though not me!

This discussion needs to be understood in its context – Joseph was not a popular boy and was rarely invited to join in the children's games at playtime. This exchange is typical of his forceful manner but, equally, Louise does not allow him to dominate her, rejecting his opinion.

It was clear that the children were using culture and religion interchangeably, especially in their answers to this question, although it provided some interesting data on the children's conceptions of culture and identity. In Rarnlow school's focus group, Manpreet, a British Asian Sikh girl, said 'So you want to find out what we think – like we're a computer with information and you click on it'. This reminded me that it did not matter if the children used religion and culture interchangeably because I was interested in what they thought.

This discussion at Deasham school between Marshall, of African heritage, and Tejpreet and John, both of British Asian heritage also consider choosing one's own identity.

Marshall: I put yes I think everyone has a culture and if you want you could be more than one and you can make your own up

Sally: You could make your own up? Make your own culture up?

Marshall: I don't know? Yeah like if I want ... Like if I want to be naughty scruffy looking that would be my own culture ... But I wouldn't, I got a *nice* culture ha ha

> Sally: Ok Tejpreet what did you put?
>
> Tejpreet: I think cultures are separate because they don't believe in the same gods and stuff like that yeah
>
> Marshall: Isn't that religions – they pray?
>
> Tejpreet: Everyone doesn't have – yeah they have I don't know about that one if they do or not ...

Marshall had a strong personality and was confident in articulating his thoughts whereas Tina, dual heritage British Asian and white, was less independent, and her father's influence on some aspects of her behaviour was evident:

> Tina: Miss I'm not allowed to eat meat on Tuesdays or Sundays
>
> Sally: Why not?
>
> Tina: Miss I don't know my dad just said it
>
> Karen: Some Sikhs on certain days can't eat meat
>
> Tina: I go to Gurdwara, I go a few times
>
> Sharish: I go to Mosque every day to read
>
> Karen: I just play! I put my feet up as well

The children in Exforth school also talked about choice. Mark said:

> Mark: Cos when I had a choice to believe in God or not I haven't chosen yet – cos I don't know yet
>
> Sally: So you say you choose your culture
>
> Mark: Yeah
>
> Jim: I think everyone needs to think of one when they're young but I think adults they need to choose like if they're going to be British Asian and what religion they're going to choose

Dual cultures and religions

Gurdeep, a Sikh boy and Amy, a Muslim girl, discussed culture and colour:

> Gurdeep: I've seen a Christian lady in the temple
>
> Sally: How do you know she's a Christian lady ?
>
> Gurdeep: Because she's white

Amy: At my sister's school there are lots of white people Miss but they are Muslim and Indians and she wears a suit everyday. Just because they have Jess's [a white boy] colour hair doesn't mean they're not Sikh

Gurdeep: Some Sikhs are white like Jess and you, but this lady was Christian and she become a Sikh

Amy: Probably half caste

The children from Rarnlow discussed identity in terms of religion and culture. Terri, a white girl, considered the concept of pure heritage. Despite adopting an antiracist stance, her use of the term 'pure' suggests superiority. Umadeep is a British Asian Sikh boy, and Chloe a white girl.

Umadeep: Everyone has a culture but some people have two cultures because they are probably mixed race.

Sally: What do you mean by that?

Terri: Dual heritage

Umadeep: Yeah because the mum might be British, but the dad might be an African or something like that. So he's got two religions.

Terri: Our caretaker Mrs Gadesby her mother is Italian and her father is Indian

Sally: You used the word 'dual heritage' – where did you learn that from?

Terri: We've actually been doing about that this morning with Mrs Gardon [headteacher] she said they call it dual heritage not mixed race

Sally: Oh I see – so why was she talking about that then?

Terri: Because a boy in our class called Div went to India and we started talking about him going to see his family and things and we started talking about different cultures and things. We know that heritage is like your family background and things, and if you've got like 'pure' heritage its just like, if you're Christian like, all the way back to your being an Anglo Saxon, you're probably 'pure'. ...

Sally: So what's the difference between culture and religion would you say?

Terri: Probably culture is maybe [pause]. Religion doesn't usually talk about the colour of the people, culture is more about the colour and the things they do, and the places and things, religion's more of the Gods and where they pray and things like that – they're kind of different

Remaining in your own culture and religion

Harvir, a British Asian Sikh girl from Rarnlow school, suggests that it is preferable to remain in one's own culture and marry within it too:

> Harvir: My uncle got married to a white person, and it's not her fault, but we Sikhs say that you should get married to the same culture as you, and people who don't, they sort of – it's kind of a sin to God, sort of. You're not meant to, but some people do, and that's their decision, and my uncle did and now he doesn't believe in God. Like, his dad, who's my Granddad – he still talks to him like that, but he just doesn't believe in God anymore.

> Sally: And, do you mind me asking – you don't have to answer any question at all, what do you think about that?

> Harvir: I think, well, because I am a Sikh it was a wrong thing to do, but because he's older than me I can't really say to him 'you're stupid, you're naughty – you shouldn't have done this'.

> It's his decision, if he's done that we can't change him and say divorce her or something like that. So what's done is done

Maxwell, a white boy from Rarnlow school, was embarrassed that he did not have a religion. Daniel, who is Black, is a Christian and Lucy, a British Asian, is Sikh:

> Daniel: Maxwell in your religion what kind of things do you do on Sunday? cos I was thinking about the people who don't have any religion what they do on umm Sunday ?

> Maxwell: Sometimes I go out and go skating or something .

> Lucy: What are you then [religion]?

> Maxwell: Normal [embarrassed and surprised]

> Sally: But do you think some people have no religion.

> Lucy: I think everyone has a religion...

Daniel's religion was so important to him that he was genuinely curious to know what non-religious people do and think. Daniel, Lucy and Maxwell continued to explore the concept of identity and considered other related concepts such as pride in one's own culture, and being a 'nice' person. This theme is picked up again later.

> Daniel: There's a movie I watched that was made in 1951 and it's called *Imitation of Life*, and it's about this girl. And her mother's black, except when she was born she turned out to be white, and she keeps on pretending she's

white, and ummm people abuse her because they find out that she's actually black. Her family's black except she's white, and she's embarrassed about that (pause). You shouldn't be embarrassed about what colour you are

Sally: Why do you think she felt she had to pretend that she was white?

Daniel: Well mainly everyone she knew was white so she wanted to be like that

Lucy: She probably didn't wanna be black, but it doesn't matter what you are.

Daniel: Having friends, it doesn't matter what colour you are it doesn't really matter – it matters about your personality really and what kind of friends you like to have

These extracts give some idea of the variety of the children's opinions about culture.

Hall (1996) proposes that identities are not static or pure but change in new circumstances as they share space with people of a variety of heritages. The corollary to this is that a new Britishness emerges to which everyone contributes. However, I do not think Hall and Modood (*et al*, 2006) would have us believe that individual cultures are vanishing, to be replaced by one homogeneous super culture. Indeed they admit that there has been a resurgence in Muslim awareness (Modood *et al*, 1997; Modood *et al*, 2006). They write about the individuals surveyed in their research who referred to themselves in terms of not only their ethnicity but also their neighbourhood, job, leisure activities and so on (Modood *et al*, 1997). Thus culture and cultural identity are to be seen as only part of a person's identity. Modood made the same point in earlier work (1992) where he discussed the ethnic minority communities' pride in their own distinctive history, language and culture and pressed for different ways of thinking: 'What we need are new concepts of Britishness' (1992:5). And he has gone some way to indicating what these might be when he later explores the impact on multicultural debates of the societal and political contexts in a particular country (Modood *et al*, 2006).

Islam in the media

Modood *et al* (1997) presented Muslims' perceptions of their own identity but Islam is presented quite differently by the mass media.

In *Islam and the West in the Mass Media*, Hafez (2000) subscribes to a radical constructivist point of view, according to which reality does not exist and so the media are 'justified in constructing reality' (2000:xii). But he is critical of the construction chosen by the media:

> Disinformation and selective reporting are more prevalent in foreign news coverage than in domestic reports, and the consumer is less able to control and supplement information received through the media. (2000:xii)

Various chapters in Hafez's edited collection point to misrepresentation of Islam by the mass media, and this was published before 9/11. The negative view of Islam which was evident in mass media reportage is more pronounced now (Modood *et al*, 2006). Especially the fieldwork undertaken after 9/11, I noticed a marked change in attitude towards Islam. There was more explicit racism, directed particularly at Muslims. The portrayal of Islam in the media played a large part in the collective perception voiced by several children in Bently school.

The White debate

Some of the wider issues such as white identity formation, and awareness of different ethnicities in teaching and learning are relevant to my findings. Back and Nyak (1993), Hans and Back (1993) and Thompson (1986) all discuss white hegemony. The term cultural hegemony, defined by Marshall (1994) involves the 'production of ways of thinking and seeing and of excluding alternative visions and discourses' (p212). So white hegemony or white privilege is the domination of white over other cultural or ethnic groups. Thompson (1986) discusses how folk cultures and sub-cultures can resist a hegemony, and Sheets (2000) discusses this with regard to schools. Both these scholars demonstrate how hegemony operates and I used their work to inform my own thinking and to demonstrate how some children's attitudes reflect a white privilege stance (see chapter 5).

Yet as Back and Nayak (1993), among many others, acknowledge, 'black people have contributed to the development of Europe over a long time' (1993:9). Thus ethnic minority culture ought not to be disregarded. Hans and Backs (1993) discuss Back's childhood memory of being asked by his teacher who he most admired and replying 'King Oliver', the black jazz trumpeter. The teacher told him there was no King Oliver (1993:23). This, Back maintains, exposes the 'Little England' mentality. Black Oliver was certainly invisible to Back's teacher (1993) and thus not worthy of admiration.

Nayak arguably gives a more balanced view (1999), warning of the implications of failing to take white ethnicity into account. She suggests that less is known about the: 'racialised identities of the ethnic majority (notably English whites) and who they are in the present post-colonial era' (Nayak, 1999:176).

She cites the murder of Ahmed Iqbal Ullah (Macdonald, 1989) by a white schoolmate, and states that antiracism should have been extended to incorporate white youth, rather than retracted (Nayak, 1999: 198). She points to the multiplicity of whiteness: 'The deconstruction of white identity became, then, a means of splicing Englishness, whiteness and ethnicity' (1999:195).

The division in society remains, whatever terminology is used, between white and 'the rest'. This prepares the ground for white privilege, discussed in the next chapter.

5

Children's stances towards cultural difference

We want a happy world ... we want white people to be kind to Chinese people and Chinese people to be kind to us. (David, Rarnlow school)

The stances children took towards diversity issues varied and were not clearcut. But they fell into five general categories.

- Same but not identical. Many children, in different ways, expressed the concept of all humans being the same but not identical. People from different cultures may have different outward appearances, different customs and beliefs but nevertheless inside they are still human.

- Politically correct. Some children expressed politically correct opinions, for example they did not use sexist or racist language or gestures.

- White privilege. The general assumption is that white western culture is normal and that all other cultures are different from the norm, thus implying inferiority.

- Important to be nice. What was important to many children was whether people are nice, moral, kind etc. This was given far more emphasis than their colour or cultural roots.

- Knowledge leads to harmony, ignorance leads to conflict. Numerous children said that they thought it was important to learn about other cultures: some also believed that knowledge is important to dispel the fear and ignorance which often lead to racist incidents and conflict.

Before discussing the children's ideas more fully, it is useful to look at the conceptual framework developed by Kincheloe and Steinberg (1997) in the US and some of the debates on multiculturalism in the UK.

These authors presented a range of attitudes towards different cultures (see Table below). I used their conceptual framework when discussing my preliminary findings with the research schools. Below is a discussion of the types of multiculturalism they identified and how the categories listed above compare with their typology.

Table 5.1 Types of multiculturalism
adapted from Kincheloe and Steinberg (1997)

Conservative multi culturalists (mono culturalism)	are tokenist. They attempt to address multicultural issues but deep down believe in the superiority of western (white), patriarchal culture.
Liberal multiculturalists	are dedicated towards working to one race. They attempt to gloss over differences in an attempt to make everyone equal and the same ('they' are the same as 'us' they just happen to be a different colour.)
Pluralist multiculturalism	Pluralism becomes a supreme social virtue, diversity is pursued and exoticised. There is cultural tourism where 'they' (as opposed to 'us') live in an exotic parallel world. eg Hanukkah is the Jewish Christmas (an example of neo-colonialism.)
Left essentialist multiculturalists	are extreme in promoting the minority culture to the extent that the dominant culture is seen as bad and the marginalised as good.
Critical multiculturalists	believe in the promotion of an individual's consciousness as a social being. They promote an awareness (self-reflection) of how and why their opinions and roles are shaped by dominant perspectives. They appreciate that there are differences within as well as between cultures.

Kincheloe and Steinberg's main argument is embedded in the critical theorist tradition of the Frankfurt school, which includes Horkheimer, Adorno, Benjamin, Lowenthal and Marcuse (Kincheloe and Steinberg, 1997:23). They emphasise that critical multiculturalism, which is their preferred type, should permeate the whole learning experience. They argue that teachers must appreciate their own 'locality in the web of reality' (p30). This relates, for example, to the white movement proponents, like Howard (2000), who discusses the need for white teachers to be aware of their own ethnicity. Kincheloe and Steinberg identify a problem for the middle and upper middle classes who have little exposure to struggle so are 'often blind to their own privilege' (p83).

Throughout their book, they refer to popular media characters to illustrate their points. We saw in chapter 1 how the media's distortion of a supposed reality can then become reality. They use television characters to illustrate another of their types of multiculturalists viewing the *Cosby Show* as an example of liberal multiculturalism. The Cosbys are a black family but lead an upper middle-class life and adopt white western patriarchal values. Thus liberal multiculturalist educators and television producers: 'speak the language of diversity but ... normalise Eurocentric culture as the tacit norm everyone references' (Kincheloe and Steinberg, 1997, p11).

The black characters in *Cosby* are rarely affected by the fact that they are black: there is invisibility or colour blindness (see Jones, 1998, 1999). This is not the case in the British television series *Dr Who*. Dr Who's black companion, Martha, is presented through critical multiculturalism. Her heritage is often commented upon, and in one episode Martha, a houseman doctor, disproves the myth that black people have difficulty learning, by reciting the names of all the bones in the hand (Davies, 2007). Kincheloe and Steinberg aim to bridge the gap between theory and practice, but in fact they merely exhort teachers not to do certain things. They disagree with a separation between education and politics:

> How is a teacher to choose a textbook or how is she to decide what knowledge to teach? These are obvious political decisions that must be made on a daily basis in the classroom. [Teachers have to constantly incorporate or reject] a multiplicity of competing ideological constructions. (p12)

Their third type is pluralist multiculturalism which Kincheloe and Steinberg consider to be the 'mainstream articulation of Multiculturalism.' (p15). It differs from liberal multiculturalism in that it focuses on the difference between cultures rather than their sameness. They discuss pluralist multiculturalist teachers who encourage the celebration of heritage by encouraging the students themselves to take pride in their heritage and to read texts from a variety of cultures. Kincheloe and Steinberg maintain that this is not enough; positive feelings and working hard do not necessarily bring about success for ethnic minority people, women, low socio-economic and other traditionally discriminated against groups.

> Pluralist multiculturalism promises an emancipation that it can't deliver, as it confuses psychological affirmation with political empowerment. (p16)

Kincheloe and Steinberg consider left essentialism as also inadequate. Left essentialists reduce races and cultures to a static essence which is 'distinct from other cultures' (p22). An example of this multiculturalism is the case of the murder of Ahmed Iqbal Ullah by Darren Coulburn (Nayak, 1999). It was interpreted as a reaction by Darren, a white boy, to the celebration of ethnic minority culture and the disparagement of white culture. Kincheloe and Steinberg argue that cultures cannot be boiled down to essential components.

Kincheloe and Steinberg's preference is for critical multiculturalism, 'dedicated to the notion of egalitarianism and the elimination of human suffering'(p24) Their theory takes up the gauntlet of black writers hooks (1992) and Gilroy (1987), who call passionately for justice and equality. Both write convincingly and eloquently about the need for teachers to realise that 'power shapes consciousness' (p25). Critical multiculturalism offers a way forward, having emerged as a wise and powerful force, imbued with the experience of age and maturity. It reveals a world riddled with domination and oppression and strives to empower all to bring about change.

Educationalists, scholars and researchers like Kincheloe and Steinberg (1997), Troyna and Hatcher (1992), May (1999) and Lewis (2005) present important ideas but these are not necessarily translated into practice in schools. Kincheloe and Steinberg (1997) may have resurrected multiculturalism but what counts is to see what the situation in schools might be. This can only be achieved through the gathering of empirical data. My study focused on children's perceptions of their own and other cultures and these are now examined in some detail.

'Same but not identical': colour blindness

Many children said they thought all humans were the same 'inside' even if they looked or dressed differently. What the children were attempting to articulate is that hierarchical and prejudicial speech and behaviour is not acceptable, that 'we are all the same', and no one should be discriminated against. This is consistent with theories of equality and discussions of white hegemony (Thompson, 1986; Marshall, 1994; Sheets, 2000). However, the reverse side of this argument is the refusal to acknowledge difference and inequalities. Few children have any notion of white hegemony and white privilege (Sheets, 2000; Back and Nyak, 1993; Parekh, 2000; Leonardo, 2005b). This suggests that the children were ignoring differences between people, thus assuming a colour blindness approach – in line with findings of Jones (1998), Connolly (1998) and Lewis (2005), who all point out this colour blindness stance.

People are not all the same because the structural, political/idealogical, cultural, institutional situations affect black people and white people differently, as argued by black scholars (hooks, 1992; Gilroy, 1987, 1993). This line of argument relates to Troyna and Hatcher's (1992:35): they argue that it is a mistake to focus on the micro level, that is, on what happens in school, between friends, at the expense of considering the macro situation where ethnic minority groups are consistently discriminated against. Jones (1999) showed how student teachers were unaware of the macro context of white privilege and that their statements that 'I treat them all the same' discriminated against the black students.

The children in my research spoke about people being 'the same but not identical' but also of the need to treat everyone with respect. Many thought that humans are essentially all the same but do not have identical cultures. Interviews from the predominantly white school, Bently, illustrate this: Nicola and Fiona are both British white girls.

> Nicola: It doesn't matter about a culture – we are all the same we're all alive and we're all people

> Fiona: I don't think it makes a difference if someone's just a different colour...
> if they've got a different coloured skin.

Thus the children were not being colour blind in that they were intentionally disregarding a person's culture and how this might affect the way they were treated. Rather, they were trying to strip away any differentiating factors that might be contributors to unequal treatment, because 'everyone should be treated with respect'. The majority of children expressed this 'same but not identical' opinion. In Deasham school Tazia and Zena, both British Asian Muslims and Rosie, British Asian Sikh, made this point repeatedly, as the following extracts from the two diverse schools demonstrate:

> Rosie: they are the same they're just a different colour to us ... they're just
> persons, people they're not like animals or something

> Zena: And I would be the same way that I always am, and I wouldn't make
> them feel low about what I said or what I did ... I think they should be treated
> the same way as other people

Two British Asian children and one white boy from the same school express similar ideas:

> Gurdeep: [I think all people are] same as me. I don't think Jesus is good or
> bad or my God is good or bad I think they are the same Hindus are [the]
> same, every culture [the same]..

> Jess: It doesn't really matter what colour you are

> Gurdeep: I don't think, he's poor I'm rich, I think we're the same

> Amy: I've got a friend she's half caste she's half English half Indian it doesn't
> matter we're all the same

During a discussion in Rarnlow school, two British Asian girls and one dual heritage girl discussed sameness:

> Francesca: ... we all have arms and we all have legs – it's just that we all might
> be different sizes and we may have a different coloured skin or lighter hair

Daniel, British African from Rarnlow school, spoke about the non-identical nature of religions but the sameness of the concept of religion:

> Daniel: I think every religion is the same except in different ways because
> every single religion has a God involved with it somehow – it must be the
> same ... errr gods are worshipped in different ways

In the following extract from Exforth school Cassie and Saz, both white children in this mainly white school, discussed sameness. The discussion is fascinating, not least because Saz was described to me as having severe behavioural problems and a teaching support assistant worked with him full time. Throughout this discussion he demonstrated astute understanding of respect and fair play. He was positive and antiracist but knew almost nothing about other cultures.

> Cassie: Because they look like Carl's dad – he's like that – Pakistani and errm he's like normal like normal like us like our culture –
>
> Saz: Everybody's normal ...
>
> Sally: What did you mean everyone's normal?
>
> Saz: I meant like everyone's the same but not really identical I think everyone should be treated the same ... People are all the same they've got umm the same hearts and that. Everything's the same inside them it's just where they come from that gives them different skin colour ...

Cassie offered an explanation for everyone being the same but not identical: she had some black relatives. This led Saz to contradict her evolution theory and to offer a fundamentalist explanation for the origin of humans. Saz was one of only two children to write 'Christian' as his religion on the background information sheet:

> Cassie: I don't know much about them [the black relatives] – they are really distant but I know how I'm related to them
>
> Saz: Everyone's related to everyone
>
> Sally: Are they?
>
> Saz: Yeah cos in a way I'm related to her – only met up with her when I got to X town
>
> Sally: How do you know you are related to each other?
>
> Saz: Because of Adam and Eve the first people on the planet
>
> Cassie: Yeah but I believe that my great-great-great-grandad was a gorilla or something.
>
> Sally: Do you believe that [Saz]?
>
> Saz: No – I believe that humans were humans from the start. If we did start from gorillas then gorillas wouldn't be around now. And the gorillas in cages have been there for hundreds of years. They would have evolved by now so I don't really think about it

> Sally: Have you thought that yourself or have your family told you?
>
> Saz: I saw it on Walking with Dinosaurs – something like that and history programmes on BBC 2

Saz misunderstood evolutionary theory and also misrepresented *Walking with Dinosaurs* which takes evolution as given. However the extract offers an interesting insight into his attitude and its origin.

Many of these discussions demonstrate that most children believed that humans are the same because we all share similar physical characteristics, but that we differ from each other in the beliefs we hold and the physical characteristics we have.

Acknowledging difference is not always positive, though. We see this in these two discussions. Bart, Matthew and Sophie, all of them British white, are from Bently school:

> Bart: They're ugly (giggles)
>
> Sally: They're ugly? – so you think people who aren't the same culture as you are ugly? [Bart nods]
>
> Matthew: Like Tasim cos he's umm half caste and he's a vegetarian and so we're not like him ...They [Chinese] speak different to us and, like they, they can read books different and when we speak to them – they speak English to us and they can play a bit different to us sometimes
>
> Sophie: They are strange, and they are different than us too. They ain't got the same stuff and the same religions as us

Political correctness

When considering the differences between different cultures some of the children showed awareness of what was politically correct and what was not (Garner, 1994). For example, in one interview at Rarnlow school the children spoke and behaved in non-politically correct ways. Rachel, a dual heritage Caribbean and white girl, realised this and corrected herself:

> Rachel: They [British Chinese] have round faces and their eyes are like that [pulling at the sides of her eyes]
>
> Sally: OK so you're making a gesture with the corner of your eyes
>
> Rachel: Hee hee that's Chinese. I shouldn't have done that – but their eyes look different, are kind of different

Sally: Why do you say you shouldn't have done that?

Rachel: Because it looks like, it looks really, it sounds really mean when I do it because well ... if someone like Chinese was in the room – they would feel really offended.

In another interview at Rarnlow the children were themselves politically correct but recognised that non-politically correct behaviour is prevalent. Again the target was the Chinese, who were not represented in the school:

Daniel: Some of the children there used to do this 'I'm a Chinese and I look like a dork'

Sally: None of you did that did you just now?

All: No

Daniel: I think it's rude when people do that ...What about how would they feel if Chinese people make fun of the way their eyes look.

Some of the children at Bently school were unashamedly politically incorrect. We heard Max's comments about his father's dislike of 'brown skinned people'. In this predominantly white school, the two white boys talked about other cultures. My fieldwork in Bently school took place shortly after 9/11 when anti-Muslim feeling was running high.

Johnny: I don't mind if someone's a different culture to me

Max: I don't like them unless they are people that I know – like Sikh culture, only the people that I know that I like – I don't like the Hindus, some of them, because like they don't like us. Some of them, they hate whites and that's why we hate them. And Bin Laden he's like he's a killer. He like tries to kill like British people and ermm America and umm I don't like em. So I don't like 'em unless they're people that I know

Some children also spoke about name-calling. Rachel from Rarnlow school said:

Rachel: Joe called her a Paki and then she went off crying ... cos people refer to people as Pakis as people who are Indian, and I'm not being racist, but they umm they do and the person [Joe] who called the person [the girl] ... she isn't an Indian at all she's white, so

Sally: Oh so it was a person calling a white person Paki and they weren't Pakistani or Indian anyway

Rachel: No the person wasn't even Indian either. I'm not being racist

So we can see that children were, to varying degrees, aware of what constituted politically correct behaviour and speech. As I became more familiar with the transcripts I began to notice that some children held an implicitly white privilege stance.

White privilege

Many of the Asian heritage children chose western pseudonyms for this study because they thought these would be easier to understand: thus the children assumed that white western privilege would prevail in academia. It became clear from my line of questioning that these Sikh British Asian girls were using a white Christian vocabulary because they expected this to be the language I was using and that the readers of my research would use it too. The common language of usage can be described as white Christian language.

Some of the British Asian children even described their own names as 'unusual' or 'difficult' – meaning that they were unusual, different or difficult for white people:

> Harvir: You'll never remember my name because it's long and peculiar. Because I'm different I'm Indian, Sikh

When discussing clothes Carlo, a Muslim boy at Deasham school, refers to Asian and British clothes, revealing his implicit understanding that western clothes are British:

> Carlo: Miss, Asians they wear mixed clothes, they wear everything saris, trousers, everything, their own Kameez and they wear British clothes – all kinds of clothes

Some children did differentiate and call trousers, skirts, T-shirts, western clothes: these were usually children in the highly diverse schools. In mainly white Exforth school Lisette, a white girl, told me what she knew about British Chinese people's clothing and customs:

> Lisette: British Chinese people would probably wear the same clothes [as us] because they would want to like blend in to us ... I don't think they believe in God because that's like British – like master ... at home, they might not know how to use a knife and fork, so they might bring their own chopsticks over ...

Lisette thought about this and added:

> Cos it depends what you're used to – they're used to like a chopstick, and we're used to a knife and fork

Lisette moved between the monoculturalist stance and the liberal multiculturalist: she expected people of another culture to adapt to the dominant culture but she did not want them to seem inferior.

Clothes

Kincheloe and Steinberg's (1997) types of multiculturalism (see Table 5.1, page 82) are used to analyse the example below. There were a significant number of children in both types of schools who understood that western white culture may be the dominant culture but one doesn't have to conform to it. In Deasham school Melissa, of African heritage, and Zoe, a British Asian, were discussing Asian dress and a girl in their class, Amy, who wore western clothes. Zoe was adamant that British Asians should be proud to wear traditional Asian dress if they chose to.

> Melissa: Amy's an Asian – she's an Indian and she wears proper clothes like white people, like normal people wear
>
> Zoe: It depends what you're allowed to wear ...
>
> Melissa: ... she doesn't really like wearing clothes like these [points to Zoe's] because she gets embarrassed ... that people might make fun of her, [of] what she wears because of her religion ...
>
> Zoe: Really you shouldn't be embarrassed about your own culture because that's your own culture and if people don't like it then you shouldn't really care ... you should go ahead and wear what you want and be what you want with your own culture ...

This contrasts with some prevailing views on the wearing of the niquab, the Muslim veil, and the hijab or headscarf. Weller argues that there needs to be some acknowledgement of the existence and contribution of ethnic minority communities in Europe: we do not live in a monocultural society:

> European self-understandings which exclude people of other than Christian religious traditions, either by design or by default are, historically speaking, fundamentally distorted. Politically and religiously such self-understandings are dangerous and need to be challenged. (Weller, 2000:9)

Thus being allowed or forbidden to wear the veil may be an indicator of a country's cultural tolerance. Britain, despite a few negative incidents, has moved towards greater acceptance of diversity of dress than France and Germany (*The Islamic veil across Europe*, 2006; Elton-Chalcraft,

2008a). Hammond argues against intolerance towards the wearing of the veil:

> When veiling as an act of piety stands also as a symbol of resistance against the insults of local Islamophobes and the perceived Western anti-Muslim crusade, it is not surprising that the practice is passionately adhered to and attempts to remove it fiercely resisted. (Hammond, 2006)

Colour

Despite most children in my study viewing whiteness as normal, Melissa, who was of African heritage, did not subscribe to this view. She is challenged when she describes Muslims as having light skin by Zoe, a British Asian:

> Melissa: It's not really my culture ... they go to the mosque every day – well most Muslims do ... they have light skin
>
> Sally: Light skin?
>
> Zoe: ... It's normally dark (laughing)
>
> Melissa: But it's lighter than mine cos mine is the darkest.

Melissa undermined the Kincheloe and Steinberg model (1997) of viewing the dominant culture as white western. She viewed her own culture and skin colour as normal, so she defined Asian skin colour as light. But for most of the children skin colour was defined with reference to white as the norm rather than black.

They equated British with white. The concept of Britishness was discussed in the previous chapter and this section ends by looking at Kurt's comment, where, interestingly, he talked about the literal colour of his skin. When Kurt, of dual heritage, did not want to describe himself as either black or white, he said: 'I'm orange'. Perhaps he did not want to be pigeonholed as Black and so he created his own identity: orange.

Language

A position of white privilege was reflected in children's use of the language of white western, often Christian, beliefs and values when they were describing cultures. In Bently school, two white boys described the Muslim festival of Eid by using Christian language:

> Max: They [Muslims] have like a Christmas just before ours – it's because like the moon – they always have it at different times. It's called Eid

Even the one Muslim boy in the group adopted this language, describing Muslim festivals in Christian terms:

> Johnny: Cos I have three Christmases a year- one on 25th Dec one on 17th Dec and one on Feb the [pause] 11th. (Here Johnny was referring to Eid-Ul-Fitr and Eid Mubarak' (Fisher, 2002).)

Tina, Muslim and white dual heritage, made a similar statement:

> Tina: Muslims have Eid like their Christmas to us.
>
> Sally: Why did you say Christmas?
>
> Tina: Because English have Christmas Miss and their Christmas is like [pause] it's like their Christmas really
>
> Sally : So do they have a Jesus then Tina?
>
> Tina: No miss but they have different gods

It might be that these children compare Eid with Christmas because the vocabulary is familiar both to them and to me. They may have been unable to articulate that Eid is a festival which is of great importance to Muslims because of its historical significance (Fisher, 2002) and found it difficult to describe the story behind the festival: what it means to Muslims today. Perhaps they thought it was easier to make the comparison with Christmas, which they obviously considered to be universally recognised as important. The children were assuming that Christmas was a benchmark which every other festival can be compared to. Kincheloe and Steinberg (1997) note in their pluralist multiculturalist category that: 'Hannukah is the Jewish Christmas'. I never heard a child say Christmas is the Christian Eid.

Children at Rarnlow school also use the vocabulary of white privilege: two Asian heritage girls used the word Church rather than Gurdwara:

> Monica: I come to know about other cultures because like at school I learn it from my friends and that, and from home. When I go to like church, on some days, and my family's..
>
> Sally: You go to what?
>
> Monica: Church on some days and my family like tells me about my religion
> ...
>
> Sally: Could I ask you what your religion is? You don't have to answer
>
> Monica: Sikh

Sally: But you go to church as well?

Monica: Yeah on some days – go to the Sikh temple

Sally: So you go to the Sikh temple on Sundays and you call it church

Monica: Yes still because when we say church we say *Gurdwara* but it might be like hard for like English people to pronounce so we just say church as well

Sally: Oh I see, were you just doing that for me because I might not know what *Gurdwara* meant?

All: Yeah [shyly]

Sally: If I'd have been an Asian person would you have said *Gurdwara*?

Monica: Maybe maybe not, because if others are going to hear it, they might not, if they aren't Asian, they might not understand it. They'd want to know what it meant and it's easier to say it in English ... I say like to my friends 'Oh I took Memuna to the *Gurdwara* on Sunday' cos now they all know what it means, because we talk about our religion to each other and so they know what it means.

'Important to be nice'

As prevalent among the children in my research as a privileged white position, was how important they felt it was to be 'nice' to everyone, including those from a culture different from their own. Many children also believed that it was ignorance which led to conflict and that harmony was achieved through knowledge about different cultures. This benevolent attitude can also be detected in the comments categorised in the political comments reflecting correctness. It is important to consider the words we choose to use because politically correct terminology has been successfully used to subvert its intentions; people have derided the politically correct terminology and it has not created a non-sexist, antiracist and egalitarian society.

Being nice was interpreted as adopting an antiracist attitude. In Deasham school, Melissa, Kate and Zoe described the importance they placed on being friendly and nice. It emerged that Melissa and Zoe had experienced a racist incident themselves. I found their re-telling of this extremely moving and felt honoured that they felt able to disclose it:

Melissa: I pulled Zarka's trousers down once I pulled her trousers down in there [points to classroom next door] ... Miss every day I was bullying her and everything

94

Zoe: Now we're alright with each other aren't we Melissa? But in year 4 we were...

Melissa: Year 3

Zoe: Year 4 it was year 4 last year. It used to be me and this boy called Bilal because we used to sit on this desk and Melissa was there too and she used to poke us with pencils and punch us and she used to make fun of us and our religion and so I didn't like that, I couldn't take it any more cos it had like been happening for two weeks and then I told my dad that I couldn't take it, and then my dad went into school, and he like talked to my teacher last year, and my teacher told Mrs Winter [the headteacher] and then [it got] sorted out, and then Melissa wrote a note of apology to me; and now we're friends

Melissa: Miss I don't know, sometimes, I'm very cruel to people for some reason. I've got this person in me that's telling me to do these things – 'do that and be naughty' but this other person in me is saying 'be nice Melissa don't be nasty to people' – don't know what it is. ... My sister loved this balloon, it was so nice and I popped it yesterday.

Melissa obviously knew what being nice entailed – she just found it difficult to implement!

Three British Asian girls in Deasham school raised this issue of being nice:

Zena: You should behave the same way like you behave to other people, different like cultures, as they are to me like, should behave the same.

Sally: Have any of you experienced ... people being not very nice to you?

All: Yes

Tazia: I was going home yesterday and this little girl she [was] calling something not polite and I said you shouldn't call other people and so she said to me you're one too and I said, well I really don't want to say it to you just think about it yourself if someone said it to you, and she went quiet

Some of the children suggested reasons why people might not be nice. In Rarnlow school John, David, both white boys and Alan, a British Asian Sikh boy who chose a western pseudonym, talked about the importance of being nice and why they think some people are not:

David: I just hate people who call people racist names.

John: It makes the street all not nice – we want a happy world not like umm not a sad world. We want everyone to be kind to everyone else, like Chinese

... we want white people to be kind to Chinese people and Chinese people to be kind to us

Sally: Why do you think people are ..well we've talked about racist, why do you think people are racist?

Alan: because they don't like our skin colour.

John: They look 'funny' and sometimes when they pray or something they might get laughed at – they laugh at them because ...

Alan: [interrupting] Yeah and white people laugh at Indian names.

Many children took the line that: 'I'll be nice to those of another culture if they are nice to me'. Such as the two white girls at Exforth school.

Louisa: I behave the same to people of a different culture to me if they are nice to me

Faye: I think you should treat them how you wanted to be treated

But antiracism is not just about being nice to a particular person: institutional racism discussed in chapter 1 must be avoided. The curriculum ought to include discussion of this rather than encouraging children to think solely about individual accountability (QCA, 1999).

The micro context of children interacting with each other in a positive way is important but children should be made aware of the macro context as well, as discussed by Troyna and Hatcher (1992) and Lewis (2005). This point is developed in chapter 8.

Knowledge leads to harmony, ignorance to conflict

Most children felt that it was important to learn about other cultures to promote racial harmony. In Exforth school Cassie and Saz, both white, thought that social integration is the key to racial harmony:

Cassie: I don't think it's like this country is just for white people and it's very rare to see like black people. I think it's just a country that we just like share

Saz: Cos you can't claim that one spot of the earth is to be ours ...

Cassie: I think we should have like more black people ... more white people in black areas and more black people in white areas ... then we'll get to know what they are like and it'll stop most wars

Sally: Has anyone talked to you about that?

Cassie: I've just seen all the stuff on television about wars and stuff and murders of black people in Manchester.

Marshall, a boy of Caribbean heritage from Deasham school, identified another important reason for learning about other cultures, which he tells Tejpreet, a British Asian Sikh boy:

> Marshall: It's important to know about other people's religions because if you want to go on *Who wants to be a Millionaire?* [A television game show], and he [the presenter] says 'Who was the King of Reggae in Jamaica?' and they [the multiple choice answers] go 'Bob Marley, Cliff Richard, Spice girls...'
>
> John:[interrupting] Everyone would know that – Bob Marley.
>
> Sally: Right! Are there any other reasons [for wanting to know about different cultures] apart from winning *Who wants to be a Millionaire?*
>
> Tejpreet: because at secondary school you learn different languages and go to like other countries

Many children mentioned the importance of learning about other cultures to establish cultural and racial harmony. Most gave less frivolous reasons for it, and some talked about conflict.

When asked about behaviour towards other cultures many children mentioned national and global events such as the Oldham riots and 9/11. British white girls from Bently school discussed these events:

> Fiona: On the news people who are white have been fighting with people who are Black in Oldham and Burnley ...
>
> Claire: Well there have been two incidents between two countries India and Pakistan, where people have been fighting over each other's town called Kashmir .... There's this town in India and Pakistan – Kashmir – and the Indians want Pakistani Kashmir and the Pakistanis want the Indian part of Kashmir, and people are fighting and there was fighting in Afghanistan – the terrorists were driving planes into the World Trade Centre causing over 10,000 people to die, and they were doing that because this man Osama bin Laden told them to get revenge, and whoever started it, like, that people, and they are on the run and they are trying to find Osama bin Laden and the war – lots of Afghanistan people are killed and they are living in lots of underground caves.

But the children also talked about incidents nearer to home, first-hand experiences in relation to 'behaviour towards those of another culture'. White children from Bently school related behaviour they had witnessed. Louise said:

Louise: Like umm last Friday I was going to the shop and there was this [British Asian] person there and this boy Anthony and he turned around to him and called him a Paki

Sally: And what did you do?

Louise: I just said Anthony stop being nasty to him cos you wouldn't like it if he was nasty to you

Sally: And what did Anthony say?

Louise: He just swore and went off

Sally: And how old's Anthony?

Louise: He's about 12

Sally: And do you know Anthony very well?

Louise: No but he's nasty and he beats people up

Two British white girls from Exforth school discussed a local event:

Lisette: There was once a fight in a chip shop over black and white skin, and black people aren't allowed in this country and that's what the fight was about ... [they are] allowed in this country I think it's a load of rubbish.

Leah: I'm fine with black people in our country. IT'S A FREE COUNTRY [in capitals on Bean Sheet]

Toni, of Italian heritage and also from Exforth school put forward another view:

Toni: The people on the news think they are so perfect and they think Pakistan is so perfect ohh and you're being racist. It's not always like that

Sally: So you think sometimes the people in picture A [a Muslim family] are actually also being racist to the white people?

Toni: Yeah cos they're not exactly perfect, they could, when they get home, say let's have a good laugh about them.

Toni also talked to another white boy, Spike, about what he did personally for those less fortunate than himself:

Toni: You know those Christmas boxes for Romania? Yeah well I never give my toys I ask my Dad to go and buy some new toys

Spike: It's a bit unfair getting old toys. Well it is kind of fair but if you go and buy new stuff it's even better

Toni: One of my friends came round my house when I'd got one of the boxes and I can't remember what it was but it was really good in the new fashion it might have been a yoyo and my friend goes 'Ohh my god you giving a yoyo to one of them little kids over there' and I said 'why not, you have one don't you why can't they have one?' He probably put in a MacDonald's toy or something

Cassie and Saz from Exforth school discussed episodes where they felt Asian or African Caribbean people were being racist towards white people:

Saz: Well in Sheffield the Pakistani man in the corner shop in Sheffield he ummm he was being extremely nasty to my cousin ... he was being racist – he said 'you English people you get on my nerves' ... Because we were taking too long to choose which sweets we wanted. Anyway we didn't buy any sweets from there in the end.

Mark, a white boy, imagined a hypothetical incident and in so doing revealed his stance on white privilege:

Mark: If they don't speak your language and they're walking down the street and there's an emergency they've seen yeah, and they want to talk to you about what's happened and they talk a different language, you won't be able to hear 'em, and so if they learn English I won't mind them, because I don't mind people who are just a different coloured skin. I just don't like it if they don't speak my language

Thus the children's descriptions of behaviour towards those of another culture demonstrate a variety of stances. They reflect extremes of opinion ranging from the politically correct and even antiracist attitudes of children who are aware of cultural differences and want all people to live in harmony; to children who have strong, sometimes racist opinions about those who 'are different' or whom they see as a threat to themselves or their community.

6

Children's knowledge and attitudes

My Dad's errm a racist because he don't like no brown skinned people but he does like half castes. (Max, white from Bently school)

This chapter discusses the children's cultural awareness, which is categorised as

- antiracist/positive and knowledgeable
- antiracist/positive and less knowledgeable
- racist/negative and knowledgeable
- racist negative and less knowledgeable

The concept of 'racism' is understood here as any comment, behaviour or institutional ethos, either intentional or in ignorance, which promotes one race or culture above another (Solomos, 2003). Most of children in all four schools in the study held a range of positive attitudes but their knowledge varied (see Table 6.1). The children who had racist attitudes were usually ignorant about other cultures but a few who were multiculturally aware displayed negative attitudes.

Each quadrant of the table overleaf is discussed with reference to my research findings and the relevant literature. The categories were not apparent to the children, but emerged from analysis of the data.

When the research began I had expected to find less racism in the highly diverse schools and more in the predominantly white schools. Many children from Rarnlow and Deasham, the multi-ethnic schools,

Table 6.1: The range of children's attitudes and knowledge

Antiracist/Positive

	B		A	
	Antiracist/Positive		*Antiracist/Positive*	
	Less Knowledgeable/		*Knowledgeable/*	
	Less Multiculturally aware		*Multiculturally aware*	

Less Knowledgeable/   More Knowledgeable/
Less Multiculturally aware   Multiculturally aware

	D		C	
	Racist/Negative		*Racist/Negative*	
	less Knowledgeable/		*Knowledgeable/*	
	less Multiculturally aware		*Multiculturally aware*	

Racist/Negative

held antiracist opinions and were knowledgeable about other cultures. But I found that the majority of children from Exforth and Bently, the mainly white schools, were antiracist too.

I also discovered that the depth of a child's knowledge about their own and other cultures did not necessarily correlate with an explicitly antiracist stance. There were many children who knew only a little about them and held antiracist opinions. However, I recognise that this research was not extensive, focusing as it did on the detailed discussions of a comparatively small sample of children. But as a microstudy, it offered intriguing insight into children's views on race.

Quadrant A: Antiracist/positive, knowledgeable and culturally aware

I found children who had, in my interpretation of the data, a comprehensive knowledge of their own culture and a good understanding of other cultures which led them to display an antiracist stance. Discussing children's knowledge of different cultures means talking about *their construct* of a particular culture, as cultures are socially constructed

(Bhasker, 1975; Delanty and Strydom, 2003; Hacking, 2003). I was interested in discovering the child's perception of their construct of a particular culture and the different kinds of constructions they described.

Knowledgeable children described a construct of a culture which I deemed to be deep or complex, unlike the shallow or factually incorrect construct described by children who were less knowledgeable. I found that children who had a strong awareness or commitment to their own culture were more likely to hold positive antiracist attitudes. Many of the ethnic minority children showed considerable knowledge of their own culture and displayed antiracist and positive attitudes towards other cultures. It seemed that their deep respect for their own culture led them to respect other cultures too (see Brown, 1998).

According to their self-definitions Tazia and Zena were fairly strict Muslims. Zena wore the full hijab. These Deasham girls knew about their own and other Asian cultures. In a child-led interview, they first referred to their prompt sheets but then digressed to describe their own experiences, prompting each other:

Tazia: You're not allowed to eat other, white people's meat because, in a day we have to pray five times a day and we have to keep a scarf over our heads sometimes when we pray and Muslims when it's a special Friday all the men they have to go to Mosque and pray

Zena: And the girls like have to wear long dresses and pray and go to a mosque ...

Tazia: If your hair comes out you have to cover it because you get bad luck ... And if you go to a mosque and like you need, you have to go to toilet and wudu it's like you have to like put water on you

Zena: You have to wash yourself before you go in the mosque so you have to be clean

Tazia: (at same time) You mustn't be dirty. And if you like if you like fart, miss, you get a really bad look and you have to go back to the toilet and wash yourself again.

Sally: Right...

Tazia: Ummm You know like Muslims if they swear there's a fairy on the shoulder, one is bad and one is good ... And they say that if you be, if you swear, a bad fairy writes a line down and when you go to God he repeats it

103

and says, this is what, and you say to the fairy, 'gimme the good one' and if it's three marks you will be proud and not that bad, because you have done like good stuff and if the bad one gets more than five, or three, then you are doing a cross sign he does somat to you, puni ... punishes you.

This account springs from the children's lived experiences. They shared personal knowledge and understanding of the impact of their faith on their daily lives with me and their friends. They listened to each other respectfully and supported each other, whether or not they were of the same faith. To some extent, the children in the multicultural schools learned it by osmosis it seemed, a lived experience of another's culture.

These children spoke from a position of strength because they adhered to their cultural practices, which differed from the majority culture, and were proud of their heritage. An unintentional consequence of non-assimilation is that this community becomes proud of its uniqueness and therefore respects other ethnic minority communities. Children who come from a white background and who do not have a strong sense of their cultural heritage may not have such a sense of security. Indeed, left essentialist multiculturalists who are extreme in promoting minority cultures to the extent that the dominant culture seems to be bad – what Kincheloe and Steinberg (1997) call 'inverse dualism' (p21) – can be very destructive. So white children, too, should explore their own white identity.

Quadrant B: Antiracist and less knowledgeable and less culturally aware

My research found many children in predominantly white schools who had as positive attitudes as their peers in the diverse schools. But they generally had less knowledge and awareness of their own and other cultures. What I came to realise was that most children stressed the importance of being nice. Antiracist attitudes seemed to go with a strong belief in being nice to all people, whatever their colour, gender, class or ability. Children from all four of the schools said they felt that knowledge about other cultures led to harmony and that ignorance led to conflict.

I also found white children who were judged to be 'positive and antiracist' yet knew little about other cultures. Their construct of a particular culture might be shallow or they were wrong about particular facts but they were, in principle, antiracist and were vociferous about the importance of being nice. For example, in Exforth school, Cassie and Saz, both white children, thought that social integration is the key to racial harmony:

> Cassie: I don't think it's like this country is just for white people and it's very rare to see like black people. I think it's just a country that we just like share
>
> Saz: Cos you can't claim that one spot of the earth is to be ours ...
>
> Cassie: I think we should have like more black people ... more white people in black areas and more black people in white areas ... then we'll get to know what they are like and it'll stop most wars

Some of the children suggested reasons why people might not be nice. In a discussion at Rarnlow school with two white boys, a British Asian Sikh boy was clear about the reason: 'because they don't like our skin colour' (see page 95 for their discussion).

Children's ethnicity, gender and social class can all contribute towards racist attitudes but so can their emotional maturity and academic ability (Deleyanni-Kouimitzis, 1998; Connolly, 1998). Children who were considered by teachers to be more able were much more likely to be positive towards those from a different culture from their own, and it was generally the less able children who expressed racist attitudes. Connolly found that children from low socio-economic backgrounds were more likely to be racist than those from professional families, although when I asked him whether he had looked at the correlation between more able and antiracism he said he had not (Connolly, 2004). Similarly Troyna and Hatcher (1992) considered socio-economic background but not academic attainment.

My finding (quadrant B in the table on page 102), is consistent with other research which shows that children in multi-ethnic schools are likely to be less racist than those in mono-ethnic schools (Aboud, 1988: 82). Aboud (1988) stresses that contact – children mixing together in multi-ethnic schools – does not necessarily diminish prejudice. She argues that the school has a profound influence on levels of prejudice but places much emphasis on the developmental stages in childhood and believes that children are more racist before the age of 7 and that work with children under 7 is of 'paramount importance in prejudice reduction' (1988:129). Lewis (2005:87) found that in multi-ethnic schools issues of race were likely to be openly discussed 'rather than ignored': 'racial discourse was more explicit' in her 'Metro2' school.

Children's awareness of different cultures was certainly richer in the schools with a high proportion of ethnic minority children because they learned about faith and customs from their peers. Yet the children in the predominantly white schools, although less aware and well informed, displayed relatively positive attitudes towards others. Antiracist sentiments were detected in all the schools. It cannot be claimed that children learn to be antiracist just because they know about other cultures. We see this in the children who fall into quadrant C. They are quite knowledgeable about different cultures but are negative or racist in some way. My findings support Connolly's conclusion that it is not enough for children of different ethnicities to be in the same school: there has to be active antiracist teaching (Connolly, 1998).

An ethnic minority group which few of the children in the study had encountered was British Chinese. Many children in all four schools were racist towards this group. In Rarnlow school, however, I found two children who refused to make mocking gestures, suggesting they were explicitly being antiracist and respectful towards Chinese culture, even though they knew few British Chinese people. Lucy, British Asian Sikh, Daniel of African heritage and Maxwell, white, were careful not to make offensive gestures,

> Maxwell: Yeah their eyes are longer, what I've found out is their eyes are down to there. That isn't being like horrible but they come to there. (*Indicating with his finger*)
>
> Daniel: Some of the children there used to do this 'I'm a Chinese and I look like a dork'.
>
> Maxwell: Yeah people do that
>
> Lucy: Yeah people turn their eyebrows up.
>
> Daniel: They do like that.
>
> Sally: None of you did that did you just now?
>
> All: No
>
> Lucy: No none of us put our eyes like that ... no we're just showing you ...
>
> Daniel: I think it's rude when people do that.
>
> Lucy: Yeah it is and people might get upset.

Daniel: What about how would they feel if Chinese people make fun of the way their eyes look

Maxwell: Yeah cos ours are dead short cos our eyes are only like that big.

So it was not just who they mixed with in school that made children antiracist: being surrounded by adults and children who are respectful towards everyone is what matters most. Many children were positive about other cultures, however little they knew about them, because they thought it was important to be nice and because they were being politically correct. Many of the children in quadrant B (antiracist and less knowledgeable) were in the top sets for literacy and numeracy, including Daniel, Lucy and Maxwell.

Some other children from Rarnlow school discussed their knowledge of Africa and Terri, a white girl, dispelled stereotypes:

Terri: Because in some parts of Africa you get main roads and proper houses and things and in some parts of Africa you get dusty roads and when you say Africa, everybody always thinks of the dusty roads and small huts and things like that ... I think some parts of Africa are like dusty roads and small huts and like they have to go and collect water from a well and things because they haven't got water coming from a tap. But some parts of Africa have got proper houses and because in Africa, I watched this programme the other day, and there's this big bridge in Africa, and it's like a main road and lots of cars are going across it, and so some parts of Africa are like like England basically, lots of technology and things.

Sally: And how do you know that that's what it's like? Have you been to Africa?

All: No

Terri: It's probably from television and *Comic relief* [held the previous week] and all the charities talking about other places and Africans that are really bad, but there are good places in Africa.

Chloe: They don't tend to mention about all the places that are well off

Sally: Why not?

Chloe: Because it's just like us really so ... you try to help the people that are not well off so you don't really mention the people that are

This extract is interesting in revealing how the children's stereotypical views have been created, and are certainly preserved, by the media.

Terri and Harvir raised the issue of racism during the focus group where the children worked collaboratively to devise a set of prompt questions (see the Bean Sheet in appendix). Many children spoke in favour of antiracism during the focus groups. We had decided that if they really did feel ignorant about a particular culture there would be no shame in showing that on the Bean Sheet (ie recording no beans), but Terri was concerned about this:

> Terri: If say we put no beans in for British Asians would the Asians, who may be in my interview group, feel we were being racist?
>
> Harvir: But if you don't know you don't know – I wouldn't be offended [as a British Asian]
>
> Terri: But sometimes people take it the wrong way

Terri was concerned that her strong commitment to antiracism might be at risk in an interview where she might inadvertently offend someone from another culture.

Quadrant C: Racist and more knowledgeable and culturally aware

Interestingly, some children who had a fairly good knowledge of different cultures were racist or negative about them. There appeared to be three main reasons. There is 'alien culture' racism, which Halstead (1988) calls 'gut racism'. Secondly there is 'regretted' racism, where children who were otherwise knowledgeable were racist or negative and subsequently regretted it. And there was what I call 'general bully' racism, evidenced by a known bully who was knowledgeable yet was reported as being racist towards those of different cultures. He was also described as a bully.

'Alien Culture' Racism

There were children in my study, who were generally knowledgeable but nevertheless were negative towards an unknown culture. This contrasts with the example in the previous section where Daniel, Maxwell and Lucy were all positive towards an unknown culture. Some children, from a diverse school, exemplify an instance of 'alien culture' knowledge in their stereotyping of the British Chinese. They claimed that Chinese people eat cats, dogs and snakes, and expressed their disgust. Such prejudicial attitudes towards Chinese culture are discussed by

Gittings (2005) and Hesler (2002). Tejpreet and John are British Asian Sikh boys and Marshall is of black Caribbean heritage,

> Tejpreet: British Chinese people have Chinese food and they eat with chopsticks and their faces be plain and stretched out and they don't get spots and stuff on your face

> Marshall: I don't know much about Chinese people but I know they have plain faces and their eyes are a bit weird and they usually go ... they usually eat spare ribs or something like that – noodles and rice

> Tejpreet: They have snakes or stuff like that

> John: (at same time) Not snakes do they?

> Tejpreet: Not in Britain

> Marshall: They don't eat snakes, they eat cats and dogs- that's what I've heard I could be wrong, and chickens – everybody eats chickens

This stereotyping of Chinese food preferences is echoed in another interview by two British Asian girls from Deasham school:

> Tazia: Yeah I've heard they eat with chopsticks they don't eat like proper food like we [do]

> Zena: (at same time) I've written that they have quite wide eyes and they eat frogs and snails

> Tazia: Uggg

The children who made these remarks had all been positive and anti-racist throughout my research, as one might expect from Deasham school and from ethnic minority children. Marshall was vociferous about a Rule Out Racism initiative in which the school was involved. But the school had no pupils of Chinese heritage and all six children were ignorant of Chinese culture, as they told me themselves. I none-theless found it surprising that children who were so informed about culture and had generally taken such an antiracist stance made such racist comments about a culture of which they knew nothing.

'Regretted' Racism

The racist comments made by knowledgeable children who then re-gretted them were also about the Chinese. Rachel, a child of African/ Caribbean and white heritage from Rarnlow school, made an offensive facial gesture when talking about British Chinese, which she imme-diately said she should not have done:

> Rachel: They have round faces and their eyes are like that (pulling at the sides of her eyes).
>
> Sally: OK so you're making a gesture with the corner of your eyes
>
> Rachel: I shouldn't have done that – but their eyes look different are kind of different.

I heard numerous negative comments and stereotyping about the Chinese. Some children merely described the shape of Chinese eyes; others embellished with abusive facial gestures. Yet all the other children in the interview from which I have extracted Rachel's comments refrained from making these gestures and pointed out that they knew other children did so but they thought it wrong. Rachel made such a gesture but promptly said she shouldn't have. Most negative comments and gestures came from the less able white children, but Rachel was dual heritage girl of average ability and she recognised that her behaviour was unacceptable.

Brown (1998; 2001) and Aboud (1988) both claim that younger children whose prejudicial attitudes are not challenged continue to develop racist attitudes. Rachel had remembered that such prejudicial behaviour was not acceptable so she immediately retracted it. Children and adults may often say or do inappropriate things which they later regret. But such regretted racism should still be challenged. Rarnlow school had put in place small group sessions, inspired by Mosley's work on circle time and citizenship (1996, 1998), specifically to address the kind of behaviour displayed by Rachel, and these sessions were possibly modifying negative attitudes and behaviour. This can be contrasted with the attitudes and behaviour of Roy from Deasham school, discussed below.

General Bully Racism

Only one child in the four schools researched fell into the category 'knowledgeable, but racist or negative, about different cultures'. Roy, a British Asian, Muslim pupil from Deasham school, was described by the children as a bully. The two white boys, Harry and Kilik tried to support Ashley, a British Muslim girl, who was obviously ashamed of remarks Roy had made in the group interview before, saying that perhaps the term Roy used was not really racist. In this discussion these children from Deasham school discussed the proper and improper use of terminology, especially in terms of inter-racial conflict:

Harry: He [Roy] calls white people names sometimes

Sally: Oh right. And what do you feel when that happens?

Ashley: Miserable, embarrassed in front of Muslims

Harry: Well it depends how he [Roy] uses the names – if he calls us *gora* well I think that actually in Asian that means 'whitie' they don't use it in a racist way so I think it depends how you use the word.

Hasna: *Gora*?

Harry: Like if you say somebody's black you mean it in a racist way like you say 'blackie' or something to them – to umm be horrible because of their race that is racist but if you say they're black just as

Kilik: Yeah just saying they're black

Harry: Yeah, not as an insult then I don't think it's racist

Troyna and Hatcher (1992) also discovered children in their research who said they had not meant to be racist in the choice of terms they used. Ashley told me that Roy was just not a very kind person. Roy tried to dominate the other children and domination and racism are branches of the same tree. Carlo, who was in the same group interview with Roy, told me that Roy was being a hypocrite when he said he was kind to everyone. Carlo stayed behind after the interview (Roy had run off promptly to be first in line for school dinners) to say that Roy had lied – he was not kind to people of different cultures and in fact he bullied everyone – even other Muslim pupils.

These findings contrast with Connolly's perceptions about British Asian boys whom he described as 'small and helpless' and so incapable of being bullies (1998:127), although Grugeon and Woods (1990) say otherwise. Roy's behaviour was recognised by the school as a cause for concern but I am not sure about what supportive strategies staff were adopting to modify his behaviour. Rachel was given support in Rarnlow school to deal with her aggressive behaviour and afforded more 'dignity and respect' (Blair, 1999:20) than Melissa was. Consequently Rachel exhibited more respectful behaviour.

Quadrant D: Racist and less knowledgeable

In instances where children were negative or explicitly racist many knew little about other cultures. Four racist themes emerge from the data:

- ▣ Misconceptions – for example 'Bin Laden is a Hindu'
- ▣ Alien culture – a child's pejorative description of an unfamiliar culture or religion
- ▣ Stereotyping – children often used stereotypes when discussing their own and other cultures
- ▣ No knowledge – examples of the child saying they know nothing about a particular culture or religion

The children in category D were often the youngest I spoke to in the four schools, and generally white and not very able. Many were influenced by their parents or were reacting to events discussed in the media. This is consistent with other research (Cortes, 1995; Brown, 1998; 2001; Connolly, 1998).

I coded the following extract from Bently school under both 'alien culture' and 'misconceptions'. Max and Jeremy, both British white, made the following comments:

> Max: My dad's ermm a racist because he don't like no brown skinned people but he does like half caste cos there's a wrestler that's half caste De Roc
>
> Sally: So how did you describe your dad, your Dad's a what?
>
> Max: Err a racist he don't like brown skinned people but he does like half castes, cos he's just fine with half castes, cos he used to take the rip out of half castes but I said 'don't dad because it's a bit nasty but you can take the rip out of Hindus because I don't like them'. Cos it's Bin Laden he's like the boss of all the Hindus. That's about all I know

In the same interview Max said that his father did not like Bin Laden because of the destruction of the twin towers in America and also because he was brown skinned. This extract features a description of a culture which was alien to the child and demonstrates lack of knowledge, such as the misconception that Bin Laden is Hindu. These comments were the nearest to overt racism that I encountered in my research. All came from Bently school and mostly from less able white boys. This leads me to a tentative conclusion that boys in predominantly white schools who are not middle class nor in the more able sets were more likely to express racist attitudes towards those of a different culture.

Max expressed views held by his parents and opinions he had heard in the media. He echoes the boy in Troyna and Hatcher's research who 'tries out' the racist views of his grandmother, thus distancing himself from them: 'he protect[s] himself from any personal criticism while he sees how well the ideas 'work' in debate' (1992:131).

Max may also have been trying out views when he referred to his father's views about a proposed school visit to the local mosque:

> Max: My dad says like errmm 'I'm not going to let you go to a mosque be-cause it's not for your type and it's only Pakis that go, and because my Dad doesn't like 'em

Data coded at the 'alien culture' node (see appendix, page 148) denoted instances when I felt children had expressed opinions which had sprung from 'the heart'. This reflects the work of Halstead (1988) who categorises 'types' of racism, including pre-reflective (which includes gut-racism), post-reflective, cultural, institutional, paternalistic and colour-blind. Halstead claims that some forms of racism could be un-intentional. The 'alien culture' extracts correspond to Halstead's 'gut reaction' racism, which is pre-reflective.

I coded numerous examples of 'pre-reflective' or 'gut racism' under 'alien culture' such as the boys' views about Chinese eating habits. Also Bart, a white boy, describes Asians as 'horrible'. In one interview at the predominantly white school Bently, Bart, Michelle, both British white, and Kurt, dual heritage Caribbean and white, are discussing their know-ledge of British Asians,

> Sally: Bart what did you put?
>
> Bart: They are coloured
>
> Sally: Coloured ?
>
> Bart: Horrible
>
> Sa; Why did you put horrible? [all giggle]
>
> Bart: Because I don't like looking at them. They talk a lot ... Miss they wear rags, talk a lot and I don't like the look of their faces

Here Bart spontaneously expressed his feelings towards British Asians, even though he did not identify himself as a racist. In the same inter-view, Kurt, of mixed heritage, made racist remarks about the British Chinese:

Kurt: Look like they're bozeyed [giggles] they eat spicy food they wear tight clothes.cos I've seen a Chinese man and he had a vest, T shirt and it was dead tight on him

Kurt continued along these lines in his answer to 'what do you think about people of a different culture?'

Kurt: They're ugly [giggles]

Sally: They're ugly – so you think people who aren't the same culture as you are ugly?

Kurt: Yeah

Sally: Why do you say that?

Kurt: Because they've got funny eyes and different to ours – ours are like that, their's are bozeyed [making facial gestures].

Bart: Yeah but Heidi [Kurt's girlfriend] is a different culture to you and everyone else in, and some people in, this thing, in this school, has [a] different culture to you but you like 'em – you're friends with 'em. So I don't know what you're pointing that for – ugly ... And so if Heidi's got a different culture to you are you gonna dump her?

Kurt: [embarrassed giggle] Nnooo.

Bart, who had himself been racist towards those of a different culture, was now haranguing Kurt about his attitudes. Thus both boys made racist comments yet expressed antiracist attitudes towards individuals. This resonates with Troyna and Hatcher's (1992) findings that some children were racist towards a particular group but antiracist towards a particular individual whom they disassociated from that group.

In the diverse schools, however, children from all ability and ethnic groups had less overtly racist stances, and their comments were more to do with the customs of a different culture which they found unusual than about an actual person. Children in these schools were more likely to state that they disliked the behaviour of the people of a particular culture, whereas those in the predominantly white schools stated that they did not like a certain person.

Max said that his father did not like Bin Laden, both because of the destruction of the Twin Towers and also because he is brown skinned. This implies a reaction to a culture which is alien to him. And his remarks reveal his misconception that Bin Laden is a Hindu. This led to

114

me to believe that boys in predominantly white schools who were not in a high socio-economic group or in the more able sets were more likely to express negative attitudes towards those of a different culture. The children in Bently school were mainly 9 years old because the research was conducted in the Autumn term (at the start of Year 5); whereas in Exforth school most of the children had already turned 10 because the research took place in the summer term. Brown, however, argues that it is in the early years that discrimination is learnt but that schools offer the possibility to 'unlearn' prejudice and discrimination (2008).

The destruction of the Twin Towers generated much Islamaphobia in the media, and this had been re-enforced by many of the Bently children's families. But in the diverse schools children from all ability and ethnic groups displayed less overtly racist stances and even their spontaneous negative comments, are more to do with customs of a different culture which the speaker finds unusual, than with an actual person. Consistent with theories of prejudice presented by Adorno *et al* (1950) and Aboud (1988), the few children who expressed negative/racist views, in D quadrant, appeared to have a stratified view of society, with British white culture seen as superior and others, particularly those with which they were unfamiliar, seen as inferior.

7

The influence of the school

We don't do RE if it's sunny – we do PE outside. (Stuart: Exforth school)

The diversity of the children's thoughts and beliefs was intriguing and I was curious to discover what might have influenced their knowledge about, and attitudes towards, other cultures. Evidence for these influences can be extracted from what the children actually said. I looked at four possible influences: the school including both the hidden and formal curriculum; acquaintances and close friends and peers; parents; and television, videos and films. I realise that there may be many more but these were the ones mentioned by the children or deduced from the data.

This chapter explores the impact of the school on children's cultural development, looking at:

■ the organisation of the education system and curriculum

■ the formal curriculum, particularly RE, PSHE (personal social and health education) and school assemblies

■ the hidden curriculum

I sought to determine how much the schools promote a multicultural Britain, what Kincheloe and Steinberg (1997) call a monocultural white western standpoint, and how children's multicultural awareness is affected by the school's position.

The children talked about the influence of their school, their parents and friends and of the media on their cultural awareness. But I con-

117

centrated on the school because cultures of oppression have institutional settings, and both the curriculum and the ethos of each school appeared to provide a climate for the children's positive or negative attitudes to thrive or else to remain unchallenged. The teacher/child relationship might well contribute to the formation of a child's attitudes towards different cultures, and the oppression and domination of children is linked with racism (Lewis, 2005). Teachers' attitudes towards lessons such as RE are discussed – and so are their attitudes towards the children.

Organisation of the curriculum

In England there are different types of schools and currently parents can to some extent choose a school for their child from among community schools and various types of faith-based schools (Francis and Lankshear, 1993; Parker-Jenkins *et al*, 2005; Surrey CC, 2007). The School Standards and Framework Act (1998) created four categories of schools within the state system in England and Wales:

- Community schools (formerly County schools)
- Foundation schools (formerly Grant Maintained schools)
- Voluntary Aided schools
- Voluntary controlled schools

(Parker-Jenkins *et al*, 2005:17)

Parents can also choose to send their children to fee-paying schools which, by their nature, usually exclude children from low socioeconomic backgrounds, although scholarships are sometimes available (Independent School, 2007). The four schools in this study were all community schools.

Testing

The curriculum and assessment required of schools has been seen as contributing to racism (Dadzie, 2000; Blair *et al*, 1999; Multiverse, 2009). Mrs Winter, headteacher of Deasham school, voiced her dissatisfaction with government testing of literacy standards at KS1 (6 year-olds):

> They are more interested in what the children can't do rather than seeing what they *are* capable of. I have tried for years to explain that these children [from ethnic minority families] are more intelligent because they can speak

two or sometimes more languages. There seems to be no recognition of what they can do.

In 2006 Maths and Science SATs papers were translated into languages other than English for the first time so that children for whom English is not their first language were not penalised. Their knowledge of Maths and Science was being tested, not their proficiency in English.

However, the emphasis in England on a literacy and numeracy-based morning (QCA, 1999) means that other subjects seem less important because they are relegated to the afternoon, when children may be tired. Learning about global citizenship and antiracist education can be forgotten unless the school actively promotes these issues. This was certainly the case at Exforth school, where no RE took place during the second half of the summer term.

The formal curriculum

So what opportunities exist for antiracist, multicultural and intercultural education in lessons? The design of the formal curriculum is claimed by many to support white privilege (Heldke and O'Connor, 2004; Howard, 2004; Leonardo, 2005a and 2005b; Lewis, 2005). Religious Education is a curriculum subject which allows for the exploration of cultural differences. The government is not asking that children with a religious faith should leave their convictions outside the door as they enter the neutral ground of the RE classroom, but rather that children and teachers are to critically engage with all beliefs in an open way, so that no belief is thought of as superior to another. But Christianity is still dominant in terms of teaching time and this gives the impression that Christianity is more important than other beliefs. This is an ongoing debate: (see Francis and Lankshear, 1993; Parker-Jenkins et al, 2005). This ambiguity suffuses the climate in which children are learning and within which this research is located.

I look at what the children said about what was taught and what was learnt during formal lesson time, both the operational and the intended curriculum. Three British white children recount what they have learnt at Bently school about different countries while using maps: this implies that they consider people from other cultures who live in this country to belong to another country, not to Britain. Fiona, a white girl

119

from Bently, declared: 'I learnt a lot from school because sometimes we watch videos about other cultures at school.'

The children in Deasham school talked about study days, when all the junior children went off timetable and everyone had a day of RE, often based around a particular festival from a range of faiths. Parents and members of the faith communities worked alongside teachers or acted as consultants for art, dance and poetry connected with the religious festival. Melissa, of Caribbean heritage, described one study day:

> Melissa: Then we go round in our groups and one will be art and one will be writing one will be drawing one will be making a big picture and sometimes we even get to do a dance like we do a Chinese dance and we do dances for *Divali* and *Baisakhi* as well, with sticks, and get someone to dance around you. And a teacher comes, a teacher teaches us how to do the dance – it's usually a teacher which is Indian. They know how to do the Divali dance ... I asked my, our, headteacher if some people in our class ... could do things about our own religion and we asked if we could do a dance or something ... she lets us cos we really want to show what we learn about in our religion as well

In the first of the next two extracts Zena, a British Asian Muslim girl from the same school, suggested that friends and television told her more about other cultures than school, whereas Toxic, from Rarnlow school, obviously learnt a great deal from school:

> Zena: And I think it was it was on Friday we did some RE, we had a sheet and we had to order these things what's the most importantist ... that you should believe in: 'God', and 'you shouldn't drink alcohol', and stuff about that and we had a sheet about RE; and school tells you about umm cultures as well. But I think that television and friends tell you more about it.
>
> ...
>
> Toxic: And in RE – it builds information on other religions like err Muslims because I ... until I was err about 8, I didn't even know there was any other religions – about Muslims, and now I know what their God is called and how they read their *Qu'ran*

Learning about different cultures in school was not always a positive experience as three boys from Rarnlow school, Alan, of Asian heritage and John and David, both white, reported:

> Sally: So when you say school what kind of things do you learn at school?
> John: In year 4 we did India

Alan: We did the *Gurdwara*

John: We talked about all the Indian people

Alan: And when we did Indian songs white people start laughing at us

John: Because sometimes we do PE and we did some Indian music too .. This lady was making a dance to do, and everyone was laughing, because it was stupid

David: It's like the Israel one and European dance and that woman started singing and everyone, nearly everyone in the class was laughing I was one that wasn't.

I was told that no RE was to be taught to any of the year 5 classes during my six weeks at Exforth school and the subject was seldom mentioned in the school. At the beginning of my fieldwork in Exforth school, when I asked the children to list the subjects they learnt in school few mentioned RE. They seemed either not to know or to have forgotten about it. As Lisette said:

Lisette: Yeah we watched a video, I can't remember ... I can't remember what culture they were from, like Chinese Hindus or whatever. But one touched like a little piece of metal sort of thing and rubbed it on their finger like and then did the sign of the cross on their forehead

A white boy told me about the timetabling of RE:

Stuart: Well we are supposed to have RE on Friday afternoon but if it's a nice day we do games outside instead.

That it was a warm summer may explain why I was unable to observe any RE during my six week research period at Exforth. When I asked some white children from the school where they learnt about other cultures it appeared that it had not been from school:

Saz: From my granddad's house in Sheffield that's where [I learn about]most other cultures – cos we haven't been doing RE in our class for ages

Jim: [I learnt about other cultures from] my mum and television and visiting things – like China town, and we normally learn about it at school in RE, geography, science and something like that

Sid: I learn about other cultures from school. When you first came here you asked us if we knew anything about other cultures and I don't think any of us did – I didn't.

These statements re-enforced the findings from my observations, discussions with teachers and examination of the children's work.

Teaching and Learning – RE in England

The children's multicultural awareness was often developed through the RE curriculum as well as through the general ethos of the school. RE as taught in community schools does not nurture the child in one particular belief system (QCA, 2004). Children are encouraged to view different belief systems as valid and are allowed to reflect on their own beliefs, whatever they may be. In the three schools in my study where RE was given status and children were encouraged to explore different belief systems, I found more antiracist attitudes among the children – but still some evidence of racism. The worthy aims set out for RE in England are not always translated into effective teaching and learning. During the first phase of the research when I was getting to know the children and was not explicit about my intentions, I asked them about their curriculum: RE was nearly always one of the last subjects to be discussed and children in the predominantly white schools rarely mentioned it at all.

The role of the RE subject leader is important – but none existed at Exforth school. But the children, despite being the least knowledgeable about different cultures, were not the most racist. The most racist comments came from white boys from Bently school but this may have been because they were the youngest and also the least able. RE did occur in Bently school but was characterised by a Christocentric stance which was not in evidence in Deasham or Rarnlow schools, where the status of RE was also far higher.

Mr Modood, the subject leader for RE in Deasham school, regarded himself more as a mediator between the school and the community than as a curriculum leader. He saw RE as a race relations exercise rather than about educating the children about different cultures, not all of them represented in the school. And he saw himself as a mediator between the faith communities, of which he was a member, and the school with its mainly white staff and governors.

Although the research entailed only six weeks in each school, I found a clear correlation between RE and the children's knowledge of different cultures, and the degree of antiracism in the school. Patel (1994) argued that it is 'easier to implement' multicultural curriculum development than antiracist initiatives, the 'softly softly' approach being 'more palatable' for many teachers, especially in all white schools (Patel, 1994:47). My findings bore this out, notwithstanding the commitment to anti-racism declared by the headteachers of Rarnlow, Deasham and Bently schools. Not all the staff shared their views and certainly the lessons were not always antiracist.

In the predominantly white pilot school and in Exforth school, to give one small example, dating systems used 'AD' and 'BC', rather than 'BCE' and 'CE' (Before the Common Era and the Common Era). Grimmitt argues that the whole of the National Curriculum has a 'white, patriarchal, content-driven, and exam-led slant', which teachers are duty bound to abide by (Grimmitt, 2000:4). There is some acknowledgement of 'diversity' in Curriculum 2000 (QCA, 1999), but generally my research findings reflect Grimmitt's view.

The hidden curriculum

The hidden curriculum or the ethos of the school strongly influenced the children's multicultural development, as we saw in my account in chapters 2 and 3 of the relationships between staff and children, lunch-times and playtimes, curriculum issues, children's background information sheets. Together these are what create the school's ethos, along with attitudes to dress and language. The researcher has the advantage of seeing the bigger picture (Giddens, 1987:5-12). I could theorise from analysis of the data on these matters from all four schools.

Relationships between staff and children

In chapters 2 and 3 I attempted to show how teachers' comments and ways of communicating with children had a bearing on the children's multicultural awareness. I believe that the teachers' view of children (James, 1995) and the way they behave towards children can be linked with a domineering ethos (Devine, 2003). Thus if adults see children as inferior, children learn that inferiority and superiority exist. This notion can then be applied to different cultures being superior or inferior (see Adorno et al, 1950; Aboud, 1988).

In Rarnlow school, Mr Denton had his favourites, whom he encouraged and praised and only mildly rebuked, if at all, for misdemeanours which evoked his criticism when others behaved similarly. Mr Denton appeared to be a caring and competent teacher, but he did not treat the children with equal respect. Human beings naturally have preferences for certain types of people, usually those who are more like themselves, but teachers should ensure that they at least appear to treat children with equal respect. This is a requirement of the QTS Standards (TDA, 2007) and a recommendation for all QTS student teachers.

In Deasham school Mrs Moser did not treat the misdemeanours of Melissa, a girl of Caribbean heritage, with the same leniency as she did those of other children. In fact both she and Mr Millan seemed highly intolerant of Melissa. Although the stereotyping could not be described as excessive, there were a few isolated incidents where teacher expectations were not value free. This contrasted with the treatment of Rachel, an African heritage girl in Rarnlow school, whose behaviour had been recognised as 'disruptive' but who was offered support in the form of 'sharing sessions' with other children, along the lines suggested by Mosley (1996, 1998). The treatment of these two girls, both in diverse schools, indicates Rarnlow school's more egalitarian ethos than Deasham. This was an isolated case but I could find no evidence of support for Roy, another challenging child in Deasham who exhibited aggressive and domineering behaviour.

The turnover of headteachers and staff in Exforth affected the relationships between staff and children. During the period of my research there were three headteachers and two of the four staff teaching Year 5 children were supply teachers. The instability of staffing at the school led to an ethos of authoritarianism in the efforts to achieve and maintain discipline. There had been an arson attack on the school by a former pupil the previous year and several members of staff treated children as though they were soldiers in an army being told what to do, rather than children in a school engaging in learning. In some classrooms the atmosphere was tense. The domination of children meant they were not always respected, as we see in the case of Toni, white and of Italian heritage; a thoughtful boy who was nonetheless repeatedly reprimanded in the classroom.

Schools sometimes experience periods of change and Bently school had gone through a difficult time a few years earlier. It had implemented a behaviour policy which had made a significant difference. Many staff had productive relationships with the children. The children felt a sense of responsibility, which was not in evidence in Exforth school. But there were teachers such as Mr Benn, the special needs teacher, who were domineering towards some of the less able white boys. And it was these boys who exhibited the most prejudiced attitudes observed in the study. Lewis (2005) observed just such a reaction in her research at West City Elementary school, where 'authority and control were regularly asserted in dramatic fashion' (p42).

This suggests that the relationship between the children and their teachers can profoundly influence the way children behave towards others.

Dominating the children

Some of the children in the research schools were dominated, either intentionally or unintentionally, by authoritarian teachers and there appeared to be a link between this domination of children by adults and the dominance of white western culture. Melissa, who was of African Caribbean origin, was described by two teachers as a 'troublemaker' (see Chapter 2) and their expectations for her to act this out became self-fulfilling prophecies – as noted by Wright (1998), Blair (1998), Sewell (2000) and Lewis (2005).

The domination of superior adult over inferior child creates an atmosphere of antagonism and where the school's ethos is characterised by inferiority/superiority rather than equality, racism is set to flourish.

Lunchtimes and playtimes

Deasham school had spent time and money on resources for playtime activities. Incidents of conflict were rare and certainly not caused by boredom. Lunchtimes were civilised. Rarnlow school had a similar commitment to addressing playtime issues, and school council representatives were involved in planning an extension to the small playground. Here, too, lunchtimes were seen as a social event.

In Exforth school, however, the children were given free reign over the large play area and combative games were played, resulting in a culture of dominance where bullying flourished. At Bently school strategies were implemented to reduce incidents, such as designating 'skipping zones' and 'talking zones'. But as no running was allowed, active children were visibly frustrated. As at Exforth school, a strategy operated of 'playtime partners' but the root cause of the problems could not be resolved, namely the lack of space for children to let off steam and play in a structured, safe way. There was no possibility of enlarging the playground but perhaps staggered lunchtimes and playtimes might have helped.

Thus space and equipment affected how the schools prevented racist and bullying incidents by keeping the children engaged in safe play. And space does not necessarily prevent incidents: it can lead to the domination of one group, as was the case at Exforth school.

Dress and language

All the schools had a school uniform or school colours but this was least strictly adhered to in Deasham and Exforth. Most children at Bently wore school uniform. Many British Asian girls in Deasham wore shalwar and kameez, and many Sikh boys wore *patka* or a topknot. The cultural dress of different groups was thus explicit, whereas in Rarnlow school the majority of children wore school uniform and British Asian girls generally wore trousers. Exforth school allowed more freedom and some of the girls spoke about propriety: 'No bare midriffs or shoulders' (Cassie).

Rarnlow school's prospectus clearly outlines the recommended school dress in its uniform policy so children of Asian heritage did not wear shalwar and kameez but school sweatshirts, or tops and trousers or skirts in the school colours. As a visitor to Rarnlow school I was struck by the uniform (!) nature of the children and saw no girl or female teacher of Asian heritage wearing the hijab. The dress code was western.

The school prospectus, signs around the school and displays at Rarnlow were only in English. This contrasts with the other diverse school, Deasham, where many displays were bilingual and the prospectus was written in both English and Gujerati.

The 'hidden curriculum' thus reflected how the different cultures were implicitly or explicitly promoted or ignored. Thus Deasham school looked and felt like a multi-ethnic school whereas Rarnlow – even though ethnically diverse – resembled Bently in its conservative, traditionally western dress code. Exforth school was more relaxed over dress and playground patterns, yet the teachers were far more authoritarian in their approach to discipline. Schools should consider their 'institutional body language' (Dadzie, 2000, p39, 40) and the potential effects of the hidden curriculum.

8
Implications for practice

Everyone's the same but not really identical ... People are all the same they've got umm the same hearts and that. Everythings the same inside them, it's just where they come from that gives them different skin colour. (Saz, white boy from Exforth school)

The research has many implications for practice in schools. Education for racial equality can be delivered in various ways through effective Religious Education, PSHE, Citizenship, Geography and History programmes but there are a good many other factors that determine whether children develop open minds, a positive acceptance of diversity and a valuing of equality.

Schools need to consider their organisational goals and ensure that they

- plan multicultural/antiracist/citizenship/intercultural education and evaluate its effectiveness
- nurture pride in each child's culture and encourage respect for unfamiliar cultures
- move on beyond the 'contact hypothesis' in multi-ethnic schools to actively promoting understanding
- promote antiracist education in predominantly white schools
- start early to eradicate racism

Teachers, whatever the ethnic mix of their school, need training and commitment to

- encourage social cohesion/engagement
- challenge colour blindness
- challenge white privilege
- challenge cultures of dominance
- develop a positive mind-set and an awareness of the hidden values in the school and society

Plan multicultural/antiracist/citizenship/ intercultural education and evaluate its effectiveness

My research revealed that many schools were not engaging in any education aimed to further equality and social cohesion. Certain questions arise: Are there planned opportunities, in curriculum time, for positive discussions about different cultures and the diversity within as well as between cultures? How well are teachers prepared to lead such discussions? Are children encouraged to be positive about cultures with which they are familiar, and open to those which are unfamiliar?

There is no one definitive educational approach to promoting understanding of racial equality. There are different perceptions of what constitutes multiculturalism, multicultural and antiracist education – and these perceptions change over time. Schools need to be clear about what is likely to be effective in their school.

The issue of black-white relations is a legacy of slavery (May 1999). The debate over antiracism and multiculturalism has been unhelpful, especially in Britain, but recently multiculturalists have sought some accommodation with antiracists (May, 1999:3). The development of critical multiculturalism may replace the type of multiculturalism which tolerates people from different cultures but does not actively promote equality.

Citizenship teaching is seen by some as the successor to multicultural and antiracist approaches, but this differs from school to school and can itself be problematic. Edwards and Fogelman (1998:101) point out that when antiracists draw attention to differences between people they may precipitate antagonism. Doing nothing is not an answer, especially now that promoting social cohesion has become a statutory duty for schools. So what should schools be doing?

My research indicates that children's understanding can be developed through an ethnographic approach to cultural differences which encourages empathy with the lived experiences of a range of different communities that have diverse beliefs and practices, through, for example, lessons in RE, Geography and PSHE. Scholars support the view that this approach encourages positive attitudes towards different cultures (Green, 1999; Sanders and Myers, 1995, *100 Great Black Britons*, 2008).

Any programme should be set within an antiracist mindset which acknowledges that discrimination and prejudice towards different cultures must be challenged. This is not the same as advocating a bland acceptance of all cultures and withholding any critical analysis.

The problem, as my research revealed, is that some teachers and children find it difficult to show respect towards a culture or religion whose practices and beliefs they disagree with. But the research also showed that in many cases these teachers and pupils had incomplete – or even incorrect – information about the culture under discussion. So correct factual information must be the foundation upon which all stated opinions rest. However it must be remembered that cultures are constantly changing and definitions must likewise be fluid.

The Global Citizenship curriculum encourages critically analytical teaching and learning about different cultures (Jackson, 2003a; Jackson, 2003b; Oxfam, 2006). Children are encouraged to be proud of their own culture but at the same time critically analytical evaluation of their opinions or practices and of those which differ from their own should be allowed. Wright warns against pupils being offered merely an experiential approach, where they put themselves into the shoes of another at the expense of interrogating claims about what is true, and argues that:

> The fact that we feel good about ourselves becomes more important than whether or not we understand the world correctly. Being a contented pig is preferable to being a discontented philosopher. (Wright, 2004:171)

I question Wright's assumption that one can know the 'world correctly' but I accept the need for critical analysis of cultures. RE, Citizenship and multicultural education can work together to bring about knowledge and understanding of different cultures within an antiracist educative framework (see for example models advocated by Gaine 2005 chapter 6).

As my research showed, it was the most knowledgeable children who were able to respect the different perspectives on life from a variety of cultures with which they were familiar (see quadrant A Table 6.1 on page 102).

Nurture pride in each child's culture and encourage respect for unfamiliar cultures

Questions arise: Do teachers encourage children to be proud of their own culture whilst stimulating a healthy respect for that of others? And are opportunities provided for all children to discuss their own culture?

I found that children in the ethnically diverse schools who were proud of their own culture were the children who were respectful to other minority cultures. But it is important not to neglect the study of cultures which are not represented in the school (Troyna and Hatcher, 1992). We saw that the children in my study knew virtually nothing about the British Chinese – including the children in the diverse schools. The few children who were racist and yet knowledgeable (quadrant C in Table 6.1) were racist only about British Chinese – a culture not represented in any of the schools.

Geography, PSHE and RE lessons could focus on cultures not represented in the school: websites to support this study include Christian Aid Global Gang site (2007), Brit Kid and Euro Kid (2008). Other resources include Oxfam, 2007; DfEE, 2000; Knowles and Ridley, 2005. The use of Persona Dolls – in primary schools as well as pre-schools – can encourage children to see the similarities between themselves and those who have a different culture. They can empathise with the Doll while also recognising the differences embodied by the Doll's persona (Elton-Chalcraft, 2005; Brown, 2008).

Moving beyond reliance in multi-ethnic schools on the contact hypothesis

Are the effects suggested by the 'contact hypothesis' enough to eradicate racism and develop antiracism in multi-ethnic schools? The contact hypothesis has it that children of different ethnicities in the same school will inevitably be more tolerant of each other and get on just because they work alongside each other. This has been challenged by Troyna and Hatcher (1992) and Aboud (1988).

I found some racist children in the diverse schools and a good many antiracist children in the predominantly white schools. I discovered that there were children from these mainly white schools who displayed equally antiracist and positive attitudes to those from the multi-ethnic schools. There were more children in the predominantly white schools, however, who displayed negative or racist attitudes and one contributory factor could have been the lack of the osmosis effect (Tomlinson, 1984; 1990) or the benefits claimed for the contact hypothesis. Another may have been the prejudicial attitudes towards Muslims and anyone unlike themselves, expressed by their parents and proclaimed by the media in the wake of 9/11.

Any school can ensure that there are, for example, displays and resources which reflect our multi-ethnic society, so that no child grows up accepting whiteness as the only reality. Linking schools of different ethnic mixes has been suggested as a positive measure to promote understanding (Ipgrave, 2001, 2003b) but, as we have seen, mere contact is not enough to prevent racist attitudes and even ethnically diverse schools cannot rely on osmosis alone to eradicate racism and promote equality.

Promote antiracist education in predominantly white schools

These schools need to ask whether their pupils have sufficient regular opportunities to learn about various cultures. Whether or not the contact hypothesis has any validity whatever, children in mainly white schools may be trailing behind diverse schools in respecting cultures other than their own. This is not only because they may never encounter people of a different colour or culture to themselves. It is also because teachers in predominantly white schools often deny the need for education about racial justice and equality – what Gaine (1995, 2005) calls the stance that there's 'no problem here'. Gaine, Tomlinson (1990), Jones (1999) and Lewis (2005) have all conducted research which showed that many teachers in predominantly white schools think that multicultural education is only for ethnic minority children.

In his latest book Gaine discusses the many problems which together contribute to racism in mainly white environments. He likens them to an octopus – or what he calls the 'excusopus' (2005:172). This embodies the 'range of excuses' for 'things staying as they are'. He highlights fifteen 'excuses', refuting one of them by quoting the metaphor of 'white shoes' (2005:177) used by a Bangladeshi man who says:

> 'You people, you don't wear the shoes of racism every day, you don't know where they pinch and where they hurt. We do, but you don't ask us about them, you just keep on designing new shoes, but they're white shoes and they don't fit.' (Gaine, 2005:177)

I found that whilst many children seem to hold antiracist views (see quadrant B in table 6.1) there is no guarantee that racist attitudes will not surface when they encounter or think about unfamiliar cultures. These findings support Gaine's argument that multicultural and antiracist education is especially vital in predominantly white schools, both to overcome ignorance and to prevent potential racism.

Numerous resources are available to support teachers (Gaine (2005) devotes an entire chapter to appropriate resources). Others include Dadzie (2000), Oosthuysen (2006) *Here I am – Children from Lancashire and Around the World*, Knowles and Ridley (2005), Richardson (2004) and websites such as Oxfam Cool Planet (2007), Global Link (2007), BritKid (2008) and Multiverse (2009). On Black culture alone there is Black History month and its magazine, and websites such as 100 Black Britons. There is also the football initiative Kick It Out, with dedicated initiatives in the regions – listed in the websites in Richardson's *Holding Together* (2009).

Start Early to Eradicate Racism

Brown (2001) has shown that children come to nursery with certain attitudes already formed, and need to unlearn prejudice and racism even at such a young age. She argues that prejudiced attitudes in young children that remain unchallenged will persist through the primary phase and possibly into secondary education and adulthood.

Again, questions arise: Do early years practitioners offer sufficient and appropriate opportunities for children to learn about different cultures? And do they challenge any of the discriminatory attitudes they might express, which they have learned from the media, their families, the school or the local community?

It may be significant that the most racist children in my study were the youngest and least able (see quadrant D in Table 6.1). These children tended to display 'gut racism' (Aboud, 1988) and had not achieved the mature reflective state of their more antiracist peers. These findings resonate with Connolly (1998) and Brown (1998, 2008), who both suggest that children 'learn' to be racist and so it is important to set out to eradicate racism in the early years. Few early years practitioners have training in issues of diversity (Sure Start, 2007) but they can generally opt to attend training provided by the LA or within their own setting (*Early Years Educator*, 2007). The curriculum for these practitioners needs to provide training to avoid tokenism and learn about different cultures. They can also consult Jane Lane's impressively comprehensive manual *Young Children and Racial Justice* (2008) which covers every aspect of racism and its elimination in the early years' sector.

I was impressed by the ability to reflect that the 9 and 10 year-olds in my research demonstrated. In many cases I witnessed children's attitudes developing as they thought about issues of race and culture and it seemed as if they were 'creating themselves'. Children synthesise material into their existing web of belief which changes and adapts to new information. They have positive dispositions or negative ones towards the unfamiliar and this is where the school, and in particular the early years setting, can make such a significant difference.

Encouraging social cohesion – 'being nice'

Certain attitudes which were prevalent amongst the children and staff in my study reflected values which are often taken for granted but which need to be critically analysed and challenged. Many of the children talked about 'being nice' not just in terms of race but in general. They felt that harmony was preferable to conflict. This could be a result of schools enforcing an egalitarian message to be kind, thoughtful and respectful which is conveyed in school assemblies and through Circle time and PSHE lessons.

This prompts questions: *Do* teachers and children treat *all* people courteously and with respect, including those who are frequently discriminated against? And is social cohesion promoted in the school context in relation to different ethnic groups?

The law requires us not to act in racist ways, even when we disagree with or dislike a person's values (Race Relations Amendment Act, 2000). Many of the children in my research were naturally respectful or had learned to be respectful towards those of another culture, and many were positive about different cultures whether or not they were knowledgeable about them.

But antiracism is not just about being nice to a particular person. Schools need to consider the macro climate, as discussed by Troyna and Hatcher (1992) and Lewis (2005). It is not sufficient to think about the 'micro perspective' of bullying and racist incidents in the school. What must also be taken into account is the 'macro' situation – the institutional racism identified by Macpherson (1999). Issues of equality need to be extended beyond equal opportunities in the classroom to the understanding of the inequality that characterises society. Consequently, schools should not only encourage children to relate well with each other in school, but also to acknowledge, explore and challenge injustices that they see outside the school gates. The resources to support children to become responsible 'global citizens' (DfES, 2006), some of which have already been mentioned, should be informing the curriculum in all schools.

Challenging colour blindness

What many children in my study said in an attempt to demonstrate a commitment to equality was: 'we're all the same'. This masks their denial of the existence of white privilege. So a question arises about colour blindness: Are teachers and children colour blind and are they aware of the dominance of white Western culture?

I found that children used white Western language and normalised white Western culture. Some teachers argue that they do not want to make distinctions between children of different ethnicities because they think this itself is racist and may lead to conflict. Jones (1999) is one of many scholars to dispute this. Colour blindness denies a child's identity and may also deny that prejudice exists and may be constantly experienced. Teachers need to explore differences as well as similarities between people, but without stereotyping them or reinforcing racist sentiments. Enslin proposes a cosmopolitan identity characterised by 'openness to difference and cultural competence, the ability to relate and act successfully across cultures' (1998:155).

Gaine (1995, 2005) and Jones (1999) both point out that racism can flourish where there is a denial of difference. Different people hold different ideas, and these can be discussed. In RE, for example, children can learn about a range of beliefs about what happens after death, and then compare them with their own beliefs. *Talking Together: Conversations about Religion* (Thorley, 2004) presents conversations between fictitious children from a range of belief systems – Hindu, Christian, Buddhist, Jewish, Muslim, Sikh and no affiliation – in which they discuss names, food, appearance and death. One aim of the author is that children learn from the fictional discussions and their own to be 'sensitive to and enriched by each other rather than suspicious and intolerant of our differences' (Thorley, 2004:30).

Gaine's website also encourages children to view scenarios from a variety of perspectives (BritKid, 2008). People cannot be stereotyped to fit into a single category; some children in my research believed that all Muslims are terrorists. The concept of identity and its multifaceted nature is an important issue which can be explored in the classroom (see chapter 4) and teachers could broaden their understanding by consulting Modood *et al* (1997). 'Philosophy for children' (P4C) offers a framework for children to explore why they may be prejudiced and stereotype certain groups (Philosophy for Children, 2006). Knowles and Ridley (2005) describe work of this kind in Cumbria primary schools.

Challenging white privilege

One finding of research I carried out in England and Southern Germany (Elton-Chalcraft, 2008a) was the widely accepted view – implicitly or explicitly expressed – that white Western culture is the norm. Many of the children and adults seemed totally unaware of the concept of white privilege (Heldke and O'Connor, 2004) – the advantageous position white people enjoy and which many Black people are denied (Gilroy, 1987; hooks, 1992). So the question arises: is white western culture seen as normal and implicitly superior?

Teachers and children should recognise how white Western culture dominates the school curriculum, both formal and hidden. But no culture should be presented as exotic, one in which 'they' live in an exotic parallel universe to 'us' (see chapter 5). The organisation of the curriculum in both England and Southern Germany reinforces a white Western standpoint (Elton-Chalcraft, 2008a and 2008b) and this needs to be acknowledged and dealt with. Local Authorities, advisors, governors and headteachers need to examine their values and attitudes to ensure they comply with the Race Relations Amendment Act (2000) and use resources which promote 'whole school' approaches to tackle racism, such as Dadzie (2000) and Knowles and Ridley (2005). The curriculum, which is 'at best Eurocentric and at worst Britocentric but rarely multicentric' (Parker-Jenkins, 2005:145), needs a thorough overhaul.

Planned, regular and appropriate programmes of antiracist and global education should be provided in all schools. RE and PSHE are the obvious areas in the timetable to explore values and attitudes. But a global and inclusive perspective can imbue all curriculum subjects: see for example Coles (2007), Richardson (2009) and the BBC television series Science and Islam (Masood, 2009).

Challenging a culture of dominance

The relevant questions to ask are these: Do schools challenge domineering and oppressive behaviour, whether by teachers or pupils? Are all bullying incidents identified and dealt with appropriately?

It may be significant that the one child in my research who was racist but at the same time knowledgeable was also described as a bully (quadrant C Table 6.1). Any children who engage in racist or other kinds of bullying should be challenged and monitored. The goal is to create a co-operative and mutually respectful ethos in the school – a prerequisite for antiracism to flourish.

Identifying links between the domination of children, racism and oppression was not a part of my original research aims but nonetheless a theory began to emerge from my analysis of the data (Elton-Chalcraft, 2008a). Further research is needed to correlate these links but it is clearly important that teachers consider how they treat children. Where the climate of the school is characterised by the domination of teacher over child, or child over child, it is hospitable to racism and discrimination (Adorno *et al*, 1950; Aboud, 1988).

Teachers who regard certain children as 'inferior' and lacking in status (James 1995) create a climate of antagonism and prejudice. Some teachers I observed viewed the child as, in James' fourfold typology (1995): a 'developing child' – the child as lacking in status and relatively incomplete – allowing for the domination of superior adult over inferior child. The antagonism this view created was apparent in one of the schools I studied.

Devine's study (2003) of children and power relations in schools is also relevant. Children who are given respect and responsibility are more likely to afford respect to others. She notes that 'treating children seriously as humans in their own right' is a relatively new phenomenon (2003:2).

Children in Rarnlow, Deasham and Bently schools were involved in decision making, and all three had school councils, in which bullying was among the issues discussed. There was no school council in Exforth school, although children were involved in an anti-bullying campaign – which they told me was not very successful – so there was no forum to undermine the school's culture of dominance. Challenging the mindsets that normalise relationships based on domination are wholly compatible with the *Every Child Matters* initiative (DfES 2006a). The school climate or ethos is key. But although the DfES stressed the importance of establishing positive, respectful relationships between children and teacher, in line with the Children Act of 2004, the QTS (qualified teacher status) standards make scant reference to relationships in schools.

Develop a positive mindset in teachers and an awareness of hidden values

My final recommendation invites the question: What are the underlying values in each educational context?

The content-laden curriculum has intrinsic yet often unacknowledged values (see chapter 1). If the Primary Curriculum Review (Rose, 2008) is implemented, it too will be rooted in a set of values. Teachers cannot simply follow guidance, pick up a book, or use a resource and teach from it without engaging with the values behind the activity, because they will reflect those values in their teaching.

Willis and Ross expose these attitudes in their book for children: *Dr Xargle: An Alien's View of Earth Babies* (1988). Dr Xargles, an alien teacher, instructs his class of young aliens about 'earthlets' (human babies). For example: 'They [earthlet babies] have one head and only two eyes, two short tentacles with pheelers on the end and two long tentacles called leggies' (p3). Dr Xargles himself has five eyes and two long tentacles. He is describing another people through his own eyes and language, conveying his assured view of normality. Talk of 'us' and 'them' inevitably conveys a notion of in-group out-group (see chapter 1). In real life, it often affirms a construct of white as the norm, and a concomitant acceptance of white privilege.

All this is not to say that little can be done. It can. As Babette Brown maintains:

> Racism and other social inequalities are deeply rooted in British history and still profoundly affect the lives of children and their families. These inequalities were created by and are being perpetuated by people *so they can be changed by people*. (1998:2, my italics)

But without thought and commitment, the organisation of a school, its ethos and curriculum can allow racism to remain unchallenged. My findings demonstrate that there is no single simple problem with a single simple solution – it's not just black and white. They invite the recommendation of teaching and learning which is appropriate to our diverse society and world, that is consistent and carefully planned, and which entails analytical exploration of a variety of cultures. Teachers need to acknowledge and challenge the normalising of white culture and white privilege and to expand their own and the children's understanding of the concepts of identity and equality.

Terri, a white girl in one of my ethnically diverse schools, sums up my hopes for the future:

> Grandparents might think differently. In the olden days people seemed to be more racist. We've been brought up to know about different religions and we're friendlier ... Children know more and are less racist than adults.

Appendix
The research methods

Introduction

My research was conducted in four schools in the Midlands. In the first phase, weeks 1 and 2, I got to know the Year 5 children (9/10 year olds) in the classes from which I drew my sample. Pseudonyms are used for the children, teachers and schools (Robson, 1993; David *et al*, 2001). The children chose their own.

In the second phase I identified a sample of about 28 children from each school (with a fair representation of gender, ethnicity, socio-economic status, ability and age) who then worked collaboratively with me in a focus group formulating a series of prompt questions about their knowledge of and attitudes towards different cultures. This became known as the Bean Sheet (page 145), and the children completed it unaided, prior to the interviews. The following week they organised themselves into groups and talked about their opinions, prompted by their Bean Sheet answers, during a taped interview which was child-led rather than researcher-led.

In the short and final third phase, after preliminary analysis, I sent each school an Interim Report which itemised initial findings. I re-visited each school, apart from one which was unable to accommodate a visit from me, and engaged with staff and children separately about my preliminary findings.

Ontological and epistemological considerations
Researcher as 'Miner' or 'Traveller'

When deciding on a reliable way of collecting data I was keen to adopt a grounded theory building approach (Strauss and Corbin, 1998; Bernard, 2000). Methodologically I was influenced by both Kvale (1996) and Erricker (2001), who engaged children in conversations rather than interviewing them: they believed this to be a more powerful way of discovering what a child thinks or knows. Kvale discusses the art of interviewing:

> An interview is literally an *inter view*, an interchange of views between two persons conversing about a theme of mutual interest. (Kvale, 1996:1 and 2)

This is what I had endeavoured to achieve in my child-led research. Like Erricker, I decided to site my research in the school. This not only provided a wide range of children but was also a neutral location with a supportive infrastructure within which the interviewing could take place (Erricker, 2001). Kvale uses two metaphors to illustrate different approaches to research:

> In the *miner metaphor*, knowledge is understood as buried metal and the interviewer is the miner who unearths the valuable metal ... The alternative traveler *metaphor* understands the interviewer as a traveler on a journey that leads to a tale to be told on returning home. (Kvale 1996:3-4)

I was influenced by Bernard's idea of the empowering character of research. She describes consciousness raising with peasants in Brazil while living under oppressive conditions (2000). Bernard's idea (2000), which is akin to liberation theology (Guttierrez, 1983, 2001), is that power inequalities are addressed as she engages in research which bridges the gap between academia and the communities. She feels passionate about the participants as well as herself benefiting from the research (2000:174). I felt a strong ethical commitment to the children in my study and discussed my findings with them. In my attempt to avoid the 'smash and grab' research which Holdaway (2000:165) warns against, I involved them in every stage of the research.

Views of children: ethical issues

In discovering what the children had to say about their own culture and that of others I worked collaboratively with the children to afford them as much 'ownership' of the research as I could. My ontological perspective of the children is that they are different from but not inferior to adults – I saw them as people in their own right not as emerging or potential adults (James, 1995; Alderson, 2000, Woodhead and Falkner, 2000).

Sinclair Taylor highlights opposing views of young children as either the 'little monsters' of 'Green's Toddler Training' or the 'fantasy angels' of Mothercare catalogues (Neumark, 1997 cited in Sinclair Taylor, 2000:24) and points out that children are seldom invited to participate in the decision making processes which affect them.

One headteacher in my study argued that there is great emphasis on academic learning, and testing what children *cannot* do, so that teachers are forgetting to look at what children *can* do, and not involving them in designing the curriculum. Researchers, too, often fail to involve young subjects. As Woodhead and Faulkner note, many researchers are 'warm, considerate and humane, nevertheless when writing up [they] are objective, dispassionate and adopt the technical jargon of hypothesis testing' (2000:12).

When researching children's perspectives it is ethical to respect their 'rights and dignity, competence, responsibility and integrity' Lindsay (2000:17). I tried to apply this principle in my own research design, not only because I believe it to be ethically correct but also because it strengthened the integrity of the results.

Feminist methodology, validity and reliability

Although I did not adopt a feminist research approach *per se* (Oakley, 1981; Webb, 2000), and was not predominantly concerned with the investigation of females and liberating or empowering them, I used a methodology which had more in common with feminist than with scientific objective principles (Blair, 1998; Connolly, 1998). I did not see myself as a neutral objective observer because I knew my physical presence as a white, middle class, adult female had an influence on what the children said to me. And my pre-occupation with children not being thought of as inferior to adults also imbued my methodology with feminist approaches to oppressed groups.

Webb is disparaging about researchers who feel their presence has no influence on the data, questioning 'the surgical gloves of objectivity that appeared to prevent contamination of the research data by the researcher ... It is the methods, methodology and epistemology which determines whether a piece of research is feminist or not' (2000:36).

I noted for instance, Monica's comment about why she had used the term 'church' because she thought that I – a white, Western and presumably Christian woman would not know what a 'Gurdwara' was.

The role of child and researcher in the research process
Respect for the child's voice

Troyna and Hatcher (1992) and Ipgrave (2001, 2003a) both quote at length extracts from the children with whom they have worked. Ipgrave makes no excuse for not 'tidying up' the 'grammatical imperfections' because their expression may well be imperfect but this in no way suggests that the ideas and concepts they are communicating are ill-formed.

The art of dialogue with young children has been summed up by Wells (1986) in his metaphor of playing ball. Talking with young children is not unlike playing ball with them. What the adult has to do for the game to work is, first, to ensure that the child is ready, with arms cupped, to catch the ball; then the ball must be thrown gently and accurately so that it lands squarely in the child's arms. When it is the child's turn to throw, the adult must be prepared to run to wherever it goes and bring it back to where the child intended it to go. Such is the collaboration required in conversation: the adult doing a great deal of supportive work to enable the ball to be kept in play (Wells, 1986). At times I had to do this when a child's train of thought digressed from the discussion point.

Adopting a 'least adult role'

During initial visits I had received a mixed reception and I felt that some teachers were unenthusiastic about my research. I was acutely aware that some were not particularly keen on my being in their classrooms, and I thought that perhaps if I offered to work as a classroom assistant my presence might be less threatening and intrusive. However having read about various data collection methods (Mandell, 1991; Corsaro and Mollinari, 2000), I decided that I did not want the children to see me as an authority figure (as a teacher or classroom assistant), because this might prejudice what they chose to tell me. I wanted to assume the role of traveller (Erricker, 2001), and listen to the stories children 'chose' to tell me rather than 'mining' for specific information. So I decided not to assume a classroom assistant role but to opt for a 'least adult' role.

I was much influenced by the work of Mandell (1991) and of Corsaro and Mollinari (2000). Mandell speaks about 'negotiating entry' into the children's world (1991:44) and I did not take this for granted. I felt strongly that I needed to ask the children themselves for their consent, although I did gain consent for my research from the 'gatekeepers' the parents and schools (Celnick, 2000). I always began by asking the children if they were willing to talk to me and if they would allow me to make notes about what they said.

Unlike Mandell, I also made my motives explicit to the children in the second phase. This enabled them to contribute more specifically to the research because they were aware of its goals. Also, I felt that wholly adopting Mandell's version of 'least adult role' by pretending to be a 9 year old would provoke the children's mistrust .

In one school, the children would at first come to report incidents to me but gradually they realised that this was futile as I repeatedly advised them to go to a teacher. At the end of playtimes and lunchtimes I always lined up with the class, which the children found amusing at first but became accustomed to:

> Colin: Why are you lining up in that line?
> Sally: Because I'm working with Mr Penny's group this afternoon.

Colin was not asking 'Why are you lining up? You're an adult' but rather 'why that line, Mr Penny's and not mine, Mrs Kelly's', when I had spent my time mainly in Mrs Kelly's class.

The least adult role enabled me to view the school ethos through the eyes of a child rather than a teacher while I sat alongside them in lessons. One supply teacher in the more authoritarian school literally screamed at the children and I in my 'least adult role' empathised with them, subjected as I was to her rantings too.

It was a subjective feeling, but I noted in my journal that I felt comfortable in three of the schools but not in Exforth, where I felt scared even though I knew I would not be reprimanded. Adopting the least adult role, sitting alongside the children and lining up with them, gave me some appreciation of each school's institutional 'body language' (Dadzie, 2000:39, 40), which illuminated my findings.

However, being an adult with a non-responsible role presented an ethical dilemma at times. For example I observed Melissa at Deasham school pulling the leaves off a tree during playtime.

> Sally: I'm not a teacher – I won't tell you *not* to do something. I'll just say I really don't like the tree's leaves being pulled off. You do what you want but I don't like it.

Interestingly, Melissa stopped. Perhaps my appeal was the stronger because I was not talking to her from the authoritative position of teacher.

Throughout each of the phases of the research I constantly asked the children if they were happy to talk with me and for me to record their answers in my fieldnotes. I felt it was important to do this each time I spoke with them so as to establish that I was not superior to the child, and to confirm the 'least adult role' in terms of both my data collection and my relationship with them. It had its drawbacks, as when three boys from Exforth school refused to participate. I was disappointed because they were children I had particularly targeted but when I asked them, they just said they 'didn't want to', and it seemed unethical to probe further. The school secretary who overheard my conversation commented: 'Typical!' My theory is that I gave them one occasion where they had express permission to say 'no' to an adult.

Focus groups
In the second phase the children and I worked together in a focus group to devise a method of data collection (France *et al*, 2000). I tried to emphasise that I was interested in the children's own views, not what was said about 'culture' in books, on television or the Internet. We had similar discussions in all the schools, beginning by exploring the nature of the research process together. As Merrish, an Asian heritage girl from one of the multi-ethnic pilot schools put it, 'We are like dictionaries Miss, you can look things up in us.'

I quoted this comment in all subsequent schools as it gave the children a clearer idea of what I was trying to do. Harvir discussed the use of the Bean Sheet, and other children were inspired by the image of the dictionary, as the extracts below illustrate:

> Harvir: So this [Bean Sheet used in previous school] is not really a set of questions you are asking us but rather it's like an agenda with subjects you want us to talk about.
>
> Chloe: You're like an archaeologist trying to find things out
>
> Terri: We're like a computer with chips in our brains and you think of things you think you want to know.

With the children's input a prompt 'Bean Schedule' sheet was devised to record 'knowledge' during the taped interviews (see Table). I adapted the PRA methods (*Participatory Rural Appraisal*, O'Kane, 2000) originally used among illiterate farmers in rural locations, where the researcher measured their understanding of a concept by asking them to put some beans into a jar. I was interested in O'Kane's work because of her emphasis on PRA being seen as not just a set of techniques but 'a methodology or philosophy,' the success of which: 'lies in the process rather than simply the techniques used ... In PRA the role of the re-searcher is transparent. The researcher is seen as the facilitator of activities' (O'Kane, 2000:137).

In my research I involved the children and was explicit about the aims of the research. The PRA methods used beans which were familiar to farmers, so I decided on jelly bean sweets for the children to use to represent how much they felt they knew about a particular culture. This gave an indication of the child's perception of their knowledge (Elton-Chalcraft, 2008a).

I analysed this data qualitatively as an indication of the child's self-perception. The task concentrated the children's minds and helped them to compare their knowledge of one culture with another.

Over the course of the two pilot and four main studies, the Bean Sheet was re-fined and amended as a result of discussions with the children. This is the final version:

Table 1: The Bean Sheet – prompt questions

Name:	
School:	Class:

Date and time of interview:

3 beans = a lot   2 beans = a reasonable amount   1 bean = a little
0 beans = nothing

Question Beans	Explanation for number of beans given
How much do you think you know about British Chinese people who live in this country?	What do you know? (Food, clothes, what they do, look like, believe etc.)
How much do you think you know about British Asians who live in this country?	What do you know? (Food, clothes, what they do, look like, believe etc.)
How much do you think you know about British white people who live in this country?	What do you know? (Food, clothes, what they do, look like, believe etc.)
How much do you think you know about British African/Caribbean people who live in this country?	What do you know? (Food, clothes, what they do, look like, believe etc.)
How much do you think you know about any cultures not already mentioned who live in this country?	What do you know? (Food, clothes, what they do, look like, believe etc.)

3 beans = a lot   2 beans = a reasonable amount   1 bean = a little
0 beans = nothing

Question Beans	Explanation for number of beans given
Would you describe the people from all these different cultures as British?	NA
Do you think of 'cultures' as being separate? Does everyone have a culture?	NA
What do you *think* about people who are of a different culture to you?	NA
How do you, and others, *behave* towards people who are of a different culture to you? Can you describe any incidents about this?	NA
How did you come to know about other cultures – from school, home, friends, TV?	NA

By the end of the focus groups the children seemed to be fairly clear that they could not tell me an answer that was 'wrong' but that I was interested in what they chose to tell me based around the prompt questions on the Bean Sheet. The children were happy to complete it at home and everyone filled it in (to varying degrees) before the taped interviews. The jelly beans proved to be an incentive. Many of the children kept asking 'Can I eat the beans yet?'

Toni, of Italian heritage, had written little on his sheet and he informed me that his father had told him not to write even that much. Toni had protested, and replied that what he wrote could not be wrong because it was his ideas that I wanted, 'but my dad said: I don't want you writing any more – you are not a racist and neither am I'. The sensitivity of the whole area of race was clear. On several occasions I found myself in a difficult position morally when faced with racist comments. During the interviews, I did not comment on the racist views expressed by the children, and I felt my data was the richer for this, as this example from Bently school demonstrates:

> Jeremy: My dad says like errmm I'm not going to let you go to a mosque because it's not for your type and it's only Pakis that go and because my Dad doesn't like 'em

However, at the end of the Interim Report meeting I encouraged a discussion with the children in which it became clear that racist comments and behaviour were not acceptable. I said that I had heard racist comments during the interviews, but that I agreed with the children who had spoken enthusiastically about the 'Rule Out Racism' campaign.

Interviews

The children decided on the groupings for the interview: although some had to be re-organised due to absence, extra literacy lessons and so on.

I timed the interviews so that the children missed some lesson time and some of their free time. Most were happy to miss part of their break time as well as lessons, but I tried to ensure that they were present for the introduction to a lesson so it would be easier for them to catch up. I also tried to ensure they had some free time at the beginning or end of break. Many of the children were nervous about the interview, especially because they knew they were being recorded. I was worried lest we lose the child-centred nature of the research, which had worked so well in the first phase and the focus groups. I did not want to loose sight of my 'least adult role' during the interviews, but at first many children were quiet and nervous. After the first five minutes, however, most children did forget about the tape recorder. And it was the children who took the initiative in the interview to choose the order of the questions. Once they became used to this they happily flitted from one question to another and back again and digressed. I tried not to intervene but it did make transcription and coding of the data a lengthy process, until I found a helpful computer data analysis package, N5 (Stroh, 2000; Richards, L, 2000; Richards, T, 2000).

Analysis

Once all the interviews were over I transcribed them and coded the transcriptions. The coding took a long time but aided the data analysis as I was able to compare and interrogate answers to the same question given by children from different schools. I used N5 creatively to store extracts which I grouped together under thematic headings, called nodes.

Like Strauss and Corbin (1998:12) I did not have a preconceived idea of what I wanted to find out, rather, 'the researcher begins with an area of study and allows the theory to emerge from the data' (1998:12).

My research design follows their practice. Strauss and Corbin see an inextricable link between researcher and the data:

> Analysis is the interplay between researchers and data. It is both science and art. It is science in the sense of maintaining a certain degree of rigor [sic] and by grounding analysis in data. Creativity manifests itself in the ability of researchers to aptly name categories, ask stimulating questions, make comparisons, and extract an innovative, integrated, realistic scheme from masses of unorganised raw data. (1998:13)

I did not involve the children in the analysis stage about, for example, issues concerning the time commitment and access to the software were of concern only to me. Also as the researcher I had the advantage of seeing the bigger picture and could theorise from analysis of the data from all four schools (Giddens, 1987:5-12). The children from one school would not be aware of what I had found in another, and it was only when I returned to the school and discussed my findings with them, that the children could see a correlation between ability levels and knowledge of different cultures, degrees of antiracism, and cultures of oppression.

Choice of pseudonyms and feedback to schools

The children liked the private meeting with me where they chose their own protective pseudonym (Robson, 1993; David *et al*, 2001).This gave them further ownership of the research. I was interested to see what name they would choose. Many of the children had interesting reasons for their choice and it demonstrated the child's preference for a particular cultural identity. For example Zoe and Kate, both Muslim girls of Asian heritage, chose western pseudonyms because they said these names would be easier for the audience of my work ie a white western audience. I felt privileged at being party to their stories; this suggested that they trusted me.

I decided it was important to offer feedback because the schools had invested time and commitment to the project. They had welcomed me into the school and allowed me to scrutinise their policies and practices regarding race equality. I also saw this as the role of the responsible researcher. I discussed findings with the children as well as the teachers, and throughout the research strove to work 'with' the children, listen to what they had to say and treat them with the dignity and respect they deserve. My methodology afforded rich data and guaranteed that the research was ethical. (For a fuller account of the research design and implementation see Elton-Chalcraft, 2008a.)

Bibliography

100 Great Black Britons (2008) Available at http://www.100greatblackbritons. com/bios/yvonne_brewster.html accessed 1.8.08

Aboud, F. (1988) *Children and Prejudice* Oxford: Blackwell

Adorno T., Frenkel-Brunswik E., Levinson D. and Sanford, R. (1950) *The Authoritarian Personality* New York: Norton

Alderson, P. (2000) Children as researchers: the effects of participation rights on research methodology. In Christensen, P. and James, A. (Eds) (2000) *Research with Children, Perspectives and Practices* London: Falmer Press

Ali, S. (2003) *Mixed-Race, Post Race* Oxford: Berg

Arthur, J. Grainger, T. and Wray D. (2006) *Learning to Teach in the Primary School* London: Routledge

Asser, M. (2006) *Why Muslim women wear the veil* Available at http://news.bbc.co.uk/ 2/hi/middle_east/5411320.stm Accessed 17.6.06

Back, L. and Nayak, A. (1993) *Black Europeans? Black people in the new Europe.* Birmingham: All Faiths for One Race (AFFOR)

Bernard, W. T. (2000) Participatory Research as Emancipatory Method: Challenges and Opportunities. In Burton D. (Ed) (2000) *Research training for Social Scientists* London: Sage

Bhaskar, R. (1975) *A Realist Theory of Science* Leeds: Leeds Books

Blackburn Diocesan Board of Education and North Lancashire Methodist District (2000) *Religious Education Syllabus KS1 and KS2* Blackburn: Blackburn Diocesan Board of Education

Blair, M. (1998) The myth of neutrality in educational research'. In Connolly, P. and Troyna, B. (1998) *Researching Racism in Education – Politics, Theory and Practice.* Maidenhead: Open University Press

Blair, M. (1999) Successful strategies in Multi-Ethnic Schools: A summary of recent research *Multicultural Teaching* Vol 17 no 3 pp 18-21

Blair, M., Gillborn, D., Kemp, S. and MacDonald, J. (1999) Institutional Racism, education and the Stephen Lawrence Inquiry *Education and Social Justice* Vol 1 no 3

Border and Immigration Agency (2007) Britishness Test preparation support. *Life in the UK* Available at http://www.lifeintheuktest.gov.uk/ accessed 18.6.07

Boxill, B. (Ed) (2001) *Race and Racism* Oxford: Oxford University Press

BritKid and EuroKid (2008) Available at http://www.britkid.org/ accessed 11.8.08

British Passports (2006) Passport information Available at http://www.passport.gov.uk/index.asp and http://www.passport.gov.uk/general_rules_britain.asp accessed 12.2.06

Brooks, D. (2003) *Steve and Me: My friendship with Stephen Lawrence and the search for justice* London: Brooks Books

Brown, A. (2003) Church of England Schools : Politics Power and Identity pp 103-116 In *British Journal of Religious Education,* Vol 25:2 Spring 2003

Brown, B. (1998) *Unlearning Discrimination in the Early Years* Stoke on Trent: Trentham Books

Brown, B. (2001) *Combating Discrimination Persona Dolls in Action* Stoke on Trent: Trentham Books

Brown, B. (2008) *Equality in Action – A way forward with persona dolls* Stoke on Trent: Trentham Books

Calmeagle (2007) Poem – *People of Color*. Available at http://calmeagle.zaadz.com/blog/2006/10/people_of_color accessed 2.4.07

Canter, L. (1992) *Lee Canter's Assertive Discipline: Positive behaviour management for Today* London: Hodder Stoughton

Carrington, B and Short, G. (1998) Adolescent Discourse on National Identity – voices of care and justice? in *Education Studies* Vol 24, No 2 p 133-151

CEHR (2007) Commission for Equality and Human Rights. Available at http://www.cehr.org.uk/ Accessed 31.8.07

Celnick, A. (2000) 'Ethics in the field'. In Burton, D.(Ed) (2000) *Research training for Social Scientists* London: Sage

Christian Aid Global Gang (2007) Available at http://www.globalgang.org.uk/ accessed 11.3.07

Cole, W. O. (1994) *Sikhism* London: Hodder and Stoughton

Connolly, P. (1998) *Racism, Gender Identities and Young Children* London: Routledge

Connolly, P. (2000) What now for the contact hypothesis? Towards a new research agenda. *Race Ethnicity and Education*, 3(2): 169-193.

Connolly, P. (2004) *'Osmosis effect', 'Less able more able'.* Personal e mail exchange with author Aug 2004.

Connolly, P. and Troyna, B. (Eds) (1998) *Researching Racism in Education – Politics, Theory and Practice.* Maidenhead: Open University Press

Coombes, D. and Marshall-Taylor, G. (1988) *Come and Praise* BBC: London

Corsaro, W.A. and Molinari, I. (2000) Entering and observing in children's worlds In Christensen, P. and James, A. (2000) *Research with Children, Perspectives and Practices* London: Falmer Press

Cortes, C.E. (1995) Knowledge Construction and Popular Culture: The Media as Multicultural Educator. In J.A. Banks and C.A. McGee Banks (Eds) (1995) *Handbook of Research on Multicultural Education* New York: Simon and Schuster Macmillan

Crick, B. (1998) *Education for Citizenship and the teaching of democracy in schools* London: QCA

Dadzie, S. (2000) *Toolkit for tackling Racism* Stoke on Trent: Trentham Books

Darom, D. (1998) Humanistic Values Education: Personal, Interpersonal, Social and Political Dimensions. In Leicester, M., Modgil, C. and Modgil, S. (1998) *Values education and Cultural diversity, Vol3: political and citizenship education* London: Cassell

David, M. Edwards, R. and Alldred, P. (2001) Children and school based Research: 'informed consent' or 'educated consent' ? In *British Education Research Journal* Vol 27 No 3. Pp 347-365.

Davies, R. T. (2007) Dr Who BBC Series 3. Information available at http://www.bbc.co.uk/doctorwho/ Accessed 24.7.07

Delanty, G. and Strydom, P. (Eds) (2003) *Philosophies of social science* Maidenhead: Open University Press

Deleyanni-Kouimitzis, D. (1998) Gender roles. In Leicester, M., Modgil, C. and Modgil, S. (1998) *Values education and Cultural diversity, Vol3: Political and citizenship education*. London: Cassell

Derby City Council (2000) *Managing Cultural Diversity: A good practice guide for schools* Derby: Derby City Council

Derbyshire County Council (1999) *All Our Worlds – Locally Agreed Syllabus for RE* Derby: Derbyshire County Council

Devine, D. (2003) *Children Power and Schooling* Stoke on Trent: Trentham Books

DFEE (2000) *Developing a Global Dimension in the School Curriculum* London: DFEE

DfES (2002) *Securing Improvement the role of Subject leaders* London: DfES

DfES (2004) *Aiming High: Understanding the Educational Needs of Minority Ethnic Pupils in Mainly White schools* London: QCA

DfES (2005) Children's Act 2004, Children's Act report 2004-05. Available at http://www.dfes.gov.uk/publications/childrenactreport/ Accessed 10.4.07

DfES (2006a) Every Child Matters website http://www.everychildmatters.gov.uk/ DfES accessed 12.4.07

DfES (2006b) Citizenship the National Curriculum for England and Wales http://www.dfes.gov.uk/citizenship/section.cfm?sectionID=16andhierachy=16andarticleID=119 (Accessed 6.6.06)

DfES (2007) The Standards Site Ethnic Minority Achievement. Available at http://www.standards.dfes.gov.uk/ethnicminorities/raising_achievement/whats_new/ Accessed 11.7.07

Dilig, A. (1999) *Race and Culture in the Classroom: Teaching and learning through Multicultural Education* New York: Teacher's College Press

Donald, J. and Rattansi, A. (1992) *Race, Culture and Difference* London: Sage

Du Bois, W.B. ([1903] 1989) *The Souls of Black Folk* London: Penguin Books

Early Years Educator (2007) Information about Early Years Training and Issues. Available at http://www.earlyyearseducator.co.uk/?gclid=CO3v9c6awl0CFSdPEgod2 Sa7MQ accessed 15.7.07

Edwards, J. and Fogelman, K. (1998) Citizenship Education and Cultural Diversity. In Leicester, M., Modgil, C. and Modgil, S. (1998) *Values education and Cultural diversity, Vol3: Political and citizenship education.* London: Cassell

Edwards, V. (1998) *The Power of Babel – teaching and learning in multilingual classrooms* Stoke on Trent: Trentham Books

Elton-Chalcraft, S. (2002) 'Empty Wells? How well are we doing at spiritual well-being?' *International Journal for Children's Spirituality*, Volume 7 no 3

Elton-Chalcraft, S. (2003) You are what you wear: Female identity, fashion dress code cultural demands. *RE Today* Autumn 2003 Vol 21, No 1 pp. 18

Elton-Chalcraft, S. (2005) *ITE Using Persona Dolls in Religious Education* Available at http://www.multiverse.ac.uk/ViewArticle2.aspx?ContentId=532 accessed 20.4.06

Elton-Chalcraft, S. (2006a) Mind-set matters: Attainment Target 'Anti-Racism' in Primary RE. *RE Today* September 2006

Elton-Chalcraft, S. (2006b) 'My Dad don't like no brown skinned people' Powerpoint Presentation BERA September 2006 Warwick University

Elton-Chalcraft, S. (2007) 'RE against Racism' and 'Including the Religious Margin: Druidry, Jehovah's Witnesses and the Bahá'í Faith'. In Blaylock, L. (Ed) (2007) *RE Today Inclusive RE* Derby: CEM

Elton-Chalcraft, S. (2008a) It's Not Just Black and White: An exploration of children's multicultural awareness, attitudes and influences PhD University of Derby

Elton-Chalcraft, S. (2008b) How children see diversity – the effects of schooling in UK and Southern Germany and Implications for Initial Teacher education. Presentation to the Teacher Education Policy in Europe Conference Feb 08 Ljubljiana. Available at http://www.pef.uni-lj.si/tepe2008/papers.htm accessed 1/8/08

Enslin, P. (1998) Education and Democratic Citizenship: In defence of Cosmopolitanism. In Leicester, M., Modgil, C. and Modgil, S. (1998) *Values education and Cultural diversity, Vol3: Political and citizenship education.* London: Cassell

Erricker (2001) From Silence to Narration: A report on the research method(s) of the Children and Worldviews Project. *British Journal of RE* Vol 23 no 3 Derby:CEM

Figueroa, P. (1995) Multicultural Education in the United Kingdom: Historical Development and Current Status. In (eds) J.A. Banks and C.A. McGee Banks (1995) *Handbook of research on Multicultural Education* New York: Simon and Schuster Macmillan

Fisher, M. P. (2002) *Religions Today: An Introduction* London: Routledge

France, A., Bendelow, G, and Williams, S. (2000) A 'risky' business : researching the health beliefs of children and young people. In Lewis, A. and Lindsay, G. (eds) (2000) *Researching Children's Perspectives* Maidenhead: Open Univesity Press

Francis, J. and Lankshear, D.W. (eds) (1993) *Christian perspectives on church schools: a reader* Leominster: Gracewing

Gaine, C. (1987) *No Problem Here* London: Hutchinson

Gaine, C. (1995) *Still No Problem Here* Stoke on Trent: Trentham Books

Gaine, C. (2005) *We're all white thanks: the persisting myth about white schools* Stoke on Trent: Trentham Books

Garner, J.F. (1994) *Politically Correct Bedtime Stories* Souvenir Press: London

Garside, R. (2000) Editorial *Multicultural Teaching* Vol 18 no 3 pp 2-4

Giddens, A. (1987) *Social Theory and Modern Sociology* Oxford: Polity Press and Blackwell

Gillborn, D. (1998) Racism and the politics of qualitative research: learning from controversy and critique. In Connolly, P. and Troyna, B. (Eds) (1998) *Researching Racism in Education – Politics, Theory and Practice*. Maidenhead: OUP

Gilroy, P. (1987) *There ain't no Black in the Union Jack* London: Routledge

Gittings, J. (2005) *The Changing Face of China: From Mao to Market* Oxford: Oxford University Press

Global Link (2007) Available at www.globallink.org.uk accessed 14.3.07

Goodman, M. E. (1964) *Race Awareness in Young Children* London: Collier Macmillan

Green, J. (1999) *What do we think about Racism* Hove: Wayland

Grimmitt, M. (2000) *Pedagogies of RE: Case studies in the research and development of Good Pedagogic practice in RE* London: McCrimmons

Gross, B. and Gross, R. (1977) (Eds) *The Children's Rights Movement: Overcoming the Oppression of Young People* New York: Anchor Press

Grugeon, E. and Woods, P. (1990) *Educating All: Multicultural Perspectives in the Primary School* London: Routledge

Gutierrez, G. (1983) *The Power of the Poor in History* London: SCM press

Gutierrez, G. (2001) *A Theology of Liberation* London: SCM Press

Hacking, I. (2003) What is Social Construction? The teenage pregnancy example. In Delanti, G. and Strydom, P. (Eds) (2003) *Philosophies of social science* Maidenhead: Open University Press

Hafez, K. (2000) *Islam and the West in the Mass Media* Creskill, USA: Hampton Press

Hall, S. (1997) *Representation: Cultural representations and signifying practices* Milton Keynes: Open University Press

Halstead, M. J. (1988) *Education Justice and Cultural Diversity an Examination of the Honeyford Affair 1984-85* London: Falmer Press

Hammond, J. (2006) *On veiling* Available at http://www.multiverse.ac.uk/viewArticle. aspx?contentId=12775 Accessed 18.12.06

Hans, P. and Back, L. (1993) Black Heroes. In Back, L. and Nayak, A. (Eds) (1993) *Black Europeans? Black people in the new Europe*. Birmingham: All Faiths for One Race (AFFOR)

Heldke, L. and O'Connor, P. (2004) *Oppression Privilege and Resistance* London: McGraw-Hill

Hesler, P. (2002) *River Town: Two Years on the Yangzte* London: John Murray

Hill Collins, P. (1986) Learning from the Outsider within: The sociological significance of Black feminist thought *Social Problems* Vol 33, no 6

Hill Collins, P. (2006) *From Black Power to Hip Hop: Racism, Nationalism, and Feminism*. Philadelphia: Temple University Press

Hoffman, M. and Binch, C. (1994) *Amazing Grace* London: Francis Lincoln

Holdaway, S. (2000) Theory and Method in Qualitative Research. In Burton D. (Ed) (2000) *Research training for Social Scientists* London: Sage

hooks, b. (1992) Representing Whiteness in the Black Imagination. In Grossberg, L., Nelson,C. and Treichler, P. (Eds) (1992) *Cultural Studies* London: Routledge

Howard, G.R. (1999) *We Can't Teach What We Don't Know: White Teachers, Multi-racial Schools* New York: Teacher's College Press

Howard, G.R. (2000) Reflections on the 'White movement' in Multicultural Education. In *Educational Researcher* Dec

Howard, P.S.S. (2004) White Privilege, For or Against? A Discussion of Ostensibly Anti-Racist Discourses in Critical Whiteness Studies. *Race Gender and Class* Vol 11no 4 pp 63-79

Independent School (2007) Website offering information on the variety of independent schools in the UK Available at http://www.schooladviser.co.uk/choices.stm accessed 12.9.07

Ipgrave, J. (2001) *Pupil to pupil dialogue in the classroom as a tool for religious education* Coventry: Warwick Religions and Education Research Unit

Ipgrave, J. (2003a) *Building 'e' learning Bridges* Birmingham: CEM

Ipgrave, J. (2003b) Dialogue, citizenship and religious education. In Jackson, R. (Eds) (2003) *International perspectives on Citizenship, education and Religious Diversity* London: Routledge Falmer

The Islamic Veil Across Europe (2006) Available at http://news.bbc.co.uk/1/hi/world/europe/5414098.stm (accessed 18.12.06)

Jackson, R. (1997) *Religious Education – an Interpretive Approach* London: Hodder and Stoughton

Jackson, R. (Eds) (2003a) *International perspectives on Citizenship, Education and Religious Diversity* London: Routledge Falmer

Jackson, R. (2003b) Citizenship, religious and cultural diversity and education. In

Jackson, R. (2003c) Citizenship as a replacement for religious education or RE as complementary to citizenship education? In Jackson, R. (Ed) (2003a) *International perspectives on Citizenship, Education and Religious Diversity* London: Routledge Falmer

Jackson, R. (2003d) Should the State Fund Faith Based Schools? A Review of the Arguments *British Journal of Religious Education* Vol 25, no2 Spring 2003

Jackson, R. and Nesbitt, E. (1992) Christian and Hindu Children *Journal of Empirical Theology* Vol 5, no 2 pp 39-62

James, A. (1995) Methodologies of competence for a competent methodology. Paper to conference on Children and Social Competence. University of Surrey, Guildford, July.

Jenkins, P. (1993) *Children's Rights: A Participative Exercise for Learning about Children's Rights in England and Wales* London: Longman

Jones, R. (1998) Multicultural education is dead. Paper presented at the British Educational Research Association Annual Conference. The Queen's University of Belfast, August 27th-30th 1998

Jones, R. (1999) *Teaching Racism – or tackling it?* Stoke on Trent: Trentham Books

Kincheloe, J.L. and Steinberg, S.R. (1997) *Changing Multiculturalism* Maidenhead, Open University Press

Klein, G. (1999) 'New Approaches to Multiculturalism Reviewed' *Multicultural Teaching* Vol 17, no 3 pp 49 -50

Knowles, E. and Ridley, W. (2005) *Another Spanner in the Works* Stoke on Trent: Trentham Books

Kvale, S. (1996) *InterViews: An Introduction to Qualitative Research Interviewing* London: Sage

Ladson-Billings, G and Gillborn, D. (2004) *The Routledge Falmer Reader in Multicultural Education* London: Routledge Falmer

Lane, J. (2008) *Young Children and Racial Justice: taking action for racial equality in the early years* Stoke on Trent: Trentham Books

Leonardo, Z. (ed) (2005a) *Critical Pedagogy and Race* London: Blackwell

Leonardo, Z. (2005b) 'The Color of Supremacy: Beyond the Discourse of 'White Privilege" In Leonardo, Z. (Ed) (2005a) *Critical Pedagogy and Race* London: Blackwell

Lewis, A. E. (2005) *Race in the Schoolyard: Negotiating the Color Line in Classrooms and Communities* Piscataway New Jersey USA: Rutgers University Press

Lichman, S. and Sullivan, K. (1998) Harnessing Folklore and Traditional Creativity to Promote Better Understanding Between Jewish and Arab Children in Israel. In Leicester, M., Modgil, C. and Modgil, S. (1998) *Values education and Cultural diversity, Vol3: political and citizenship education*. London: Cassell

Lindsay, G. (2000) Researching Children's perspectives: ethical issues. In Lewis, A. and Lindsay, G. (eds) (2000) *Researching Children's Perspectives* Maidenhead: Open University press

Macintyre, C. (2001) *Enhancing Learning through Play: A Developmental Perspective for Early Years Settings* London: David Fulton

Macpherson, W. (1999) *The Stephen Lawrence Inquiry Report* London: Stationery Office

Mandell, S. (1991) The 'least adult role' in studying children. In Waksler, F.C. (1991) *Studying the social worlds of children: Sociological readings* London: Falmer Press

Marshall, G. (1994) *Concise Oxford Dictionary of Sociology* Oxford: Oxford University Press

Mason, M. (2003) Religion and Schools: A Human Rights- based Approach. In *British Journal of Religious Education* Vol 25:2 Spring 2003

Masood, E. (2009) *Science and Islam, a history.* London: Icon Books

May, S. (1999) *Re thinking Multi cultural and Anti Racist Education: Towards a critical multiculturalism* Lewes: Falmer

Mayall, B. (2000) Working with generational issues. In Christensen, P. and James, A. (eds) 2000 *Research with Children, Perspectives and Practices* London: Falmer Press

McCreery, E., Palmer, S. and Voiels, V. (2008) *Teaching Religious Education* Exeter: Learning Matters

Miles, R. (1988) Racialisation. In Cashmore, E. (ed) (1988) *Dictionary of Race and Ethnic Relations* 2nd Ed London: Routledge

Modgil, S, Verma, G.K., Mallick, K., Modgil, C. (1986) *Multicultural Education: The Interminable Debate* Lewes: Falmer

Modood, T. (1992) *Not Easy being British: Colour, Culture and Citizenship* Stoke on Trent: Trentham Books

Modood, T. (2001) Muslims. In Boxill, B. (ed) (2001) *Race and Racism* Oxford: Oxford University Press

Modood, T. (2007) *Multiculturalism* Cambridge: Polity Press

Modood, T., Berthoud, R. *et al* (1997) *Ethnic Minorities in Britain* London: Policy Studies Institute

Modood, T., Triandafyllidou, A., Zapata-Barrero, R. (2006) *Multiculturalism, Muslims and Citizenship* Abingdon: Routledge

Mosley, J. (1996) *Quality Circle Time* Wisbech: LDA

Mosley, J. (1998) *More Quality Circle Time* Wisbech: LDA

Moyles, J. (ed) (1995) *Beginning Teaching Beginning Learning* Maidenhead: Open University Press

Multiverse (2009) TDA funded site exploring issues of diversity and raising the achievement of minority ethnic children. Available at www.multiverse.ac.uk Accessed 12.1.09

N5 (2000) Non-Numerical Unstructured data Indexing Searching and Theorizing. *Qualitative data analysis program* Melbourne, Australia: QSR International Pty, Version 5

Nayak, A. (1999) White English ethnicities: Racism, anti-racism and student perspectives *Race, Ethnicity and Education* Vol 2 no 2 pp 177-202

Oakley, A. (1985) *The Sociology of Housework* Oxford: Blackwell

Ofsted (2002) *Support for Minority Ethnic Achievement: Continuing Professional Development* London: Ofsted Publications Centre

O'Kane (2000) The development of participatory techniques. In Christensen, P. and James, A. (eds) 2000) *Research with Children, Perspectives and Practices* London: Falmer

Ollerton, M. (2008) Moving from reflective practitioner to practitioner researcher. In Elton-Chalcraft, S., Hansen, A. and Twiselton, S. (Eds) (2008) *Doing Classroom Research – a step-by-step guide for student teachers* Maidenhead: Open University Press

Onyefulu, I. (1999) *A is for Africa* London: Francis Lincoln

Osler, A. (1989) *Speaking Out – Black Girls in Britain* London: Virago Press

Oxfam (2006) *Education for Global Citizenship: A Guide for Schools* Oxford: Oxfam Development Education

Oxfam Cool Planet (2007) Available at www.oxfam.org.uk/coolplanet/kidsweb/index.htm Accessed 14.3.07

Parekh, B. (2000) *The Future of Multi-Ethnic Britain: The Parekh Report* London: Runnymede Trust

Parker-Jenkins, M. (1995) *Children of Islam* Stoke on Trent: Trentham Books

Parker-Jenkins, M., Hartas, D. and Irving, B. A. (2005) *In Good Faith: Schools, Religion and Public Funding* Aldershot: Ashgate

Parker-Jenkins, M., Hewitt, D., Brownhill, S. and Sanders, T. (2007) *Aiming High: Raising Attainment of Pupils from Culturally Diverse Backgrounds* London: Sage

Patel, K. (1994) *Multicultural Education in All-White Areas* Aldershot: Avebury Ashgate

Peirce, E. (2003) *Multi-faith Activity Assemblies* London: Routledge

Penny, S. (2000) *Sikhism – World Beliefs and Cultures* Oxford: Heinemann

Philosophy for Children (2006) Philosophy for children website Available at www.sapere.org.uk accessed 20.4.06

QCA (1999) *The National Curriculum: Handbook for Primary Teachers in England Key Stages 1 and 2.* London: QCA

QCA (2000) *Scheme of Work for RE Non-Statutory Guidance* London: QCA

QCA (2004) *Non-Statutory National Framework for RE* London: QCA

QCA (2005) History curriculum Available at http://www.qca.org.uk/qca_6354.aspx Accessed 21.4.05

QCA (2006) Standard Assessment Tests SATS Available at http://www.qca.org.uk/12421.html Accessed 12.3.06

Race Relations Act (1976) Available at http://www.oxford.gov.uk/files/seealsodocs/24441/Race%20Relations%20Act%201976.pdf accessed 11.7.07

Race Relations Amendment Act (2000) Race Relations Amendment Act Available at http://www.opsi.gov.uk/ACTS/acts2000/20000034.htm Accessed 16.4.07

Racial and Religious Hatred Act (2006) Available at http://en.wikipedia.org/wiki/Racial_and_Religious_Hatred_Bill Accessed 12.07.08

Richards, L. (2000) *Using N5 in Qualitative Research* Melbourne, Australia: QSR International

Richards, T. (2000) *N5 Reference Guide* Melbourne, Australia: QSR International

Richardson, R. (2000) Lies and truths in the future of Britain. *Multicultural Teaching* Vol 19 no 1 pp 8-13

Richardson, R. (2009) *Holding Together: equality, difference and cohesion* Stoke on Trent: Trentham Books

Richardson, R. and Miles, B. (2008) *Racist Incidents and bullying in schools* Stoke on Trent: Trentham Books

Robson, C. (1993) *Real World Research* Oxford: Blackwell

Rose, J. (2008) The independent Review of the Primary Curriculum. Available at http://www.dcsf.gov.uk/primarycurriculumreview/ accessed 11.01 09

Rosenberg, M. T. (2007) *Peter's Projection vs Mercator's Projection* Available at http://geography.about.com/library/weekly/aa030201b.htm accessed 24.7.07

Sanders, P. and Myers, S. (1995) *What do you know about Racism?* Gloucester Press: London

Sewell, T. (2000) Beyond institutional racism: tackling the real problems of Black Underachievement. In *Multicultural Teaching* vol 18 no 2

Sheets, R.H. (2000) Book Reviews- Advancing the field or taking Centre Stage: the White Movement in Multicultural Education. *Educational Researcher* Dec 2000

Short, G. (2003) Faith Schools and Social Cohesion: Opening up the Debate. In *British Journal of Religious Education* Vol 25:2 Spring 2003

Shukr (2007) Website with information about Shalwar and Kameez. Available at http://www.shukr.co.uk/Merchant2/merchant.mvc?Screen=CTGYandCategory_ accessed 12.8.07

Sinclair Taylor, A. (2000) The UN Convention on the Rights of the Child. In Lewis, A. and Lindsay, G. (eds) (2000) *Researching Children's Perspectives* Maidenhead: Open University Press

Sleeter, C.E. (1995) An analysis of the Critiques of Multicultural Education. In (eds) J.A. Banks and C.A. McGee Banks (Eds) (2000) *Handbook of research on Multicultural Education* New York: Simon and Schuster Macmillan

Solomos, J. (2003 3rd edition) *Race and Racism in Britain* Basingstoke: Palgrave MacMillan

Storrey, J. (ed) (1996) *What is Cultural Studies?* London: Arnold

Strauss, A. and Corbin, J. (1998) *Basics of Qualitative Research: Techniques and procedures for developing grounded theory* London: Sage

Strinati, D. (1995) *Popular Culture* London: Routledge

Stroh,, M. (2000) Computers and Qualitative data Analysis: to use or not to use...? In Burton, D. (Ed) (2000) *Research training for Social Scientists* London: Sage

Sturcke, J. (2006) Straw: I'd rather no one wear the veil. Available at *Guardian Unlimited* http://politics.guardian.co.uk/homeaffairs/story/0,,1889173,00.html Oct 6th 2006 accessed 1.5.07

Suleaman, N. (2006) *How veil remarks reinforced its support* Available at http://news.bbc.co.uk/1/hi/uk/6117480.stm Accessed 20.12.06

Sure Start (2007) Sure Start NNEB training guidance. Available at http://www.childcareapprovalscheme.co.uk/carer/qualifications.asp accessed 16.7.07

Surrey CC (2007) Information about types of schools available at http://www.surrey cc.gov.uk/sccwebsite/sccwspages.nsf/LookupWebPagesByTITLE_RTF/Types+of+Sc hools?opendocument Accessed 10.7.07

Tajfel, H. and Turner, J. (1986) The societal identity of intergroup behaviour. In Worshal, S. and Austin, W. (Eds) (1986) *Psychology of Intergroup relations* Chicago: Nelson Hall

Teece, G. (2001) *A Primary Teacher's Guide to RE and Collective Worship* Oxford: Nash Pollack

TDA (2005) Minority Ethnic Recruitment and Retention project. Available at http://www.tda.gov.uk/partners/quality/ittprogsinitiatives/diversesociety/recruitminoritiesfaq.aspx?question=3

TDA (2006) Behaviour Management website Available at www.behaviour4learning.ac.uk accessed 20.12.06

TDA (2007) Standards for the achievement of QTS Available at http://www.tda.gov.uk/Recruit/thetrainingprocess/qualifiedteacherstatus/achievingqts.aspx accessed 12.12.08

Thompson, K. (1986) *Beliefs and Ideology* London: Tavistock

Thorley, S. (1993) *Hinduism in Words and Pictures* Norwich: RMEP

Thorley, S. (2004) *Talking Together Conversations about Religion* Alresford: John Hunt

Todd, R. (1991) *Education in a Multi cultural society* London: Cassell

Tomlinson, S. (1984) *Home and School in Multicultural Britain* London: Batsford

Tomlinson, S. (1990) *Multicultural Education in White Schools* London: Batsford

Troyna, B. and Hatcher, R. (1992) *Racism in Children's Lives* London: Routledge

Twiselton, S. (2004) The role of teacher identity in learning to teach primary literacy *Education Review Special Edition: Activity Theory.*

Twiselton, S. (2006) Developing your teaching skills. In Arthur, J., Grainger, T. and Wray, D. (eds) *Learning to teach in the Primary School* London: Routledge

Verma, G. and Pumpfry, P.(1988) *Educational Attainments: Issues and outcomes in Multicultural Education* Lewes: Falmer

Waddington, D., Jones, K. and Critcher, C. (1989) *Flashpoints: Studies in Public Disorder* London: Routledge

Webb, S. (2000) Feminist methodology. In Burton, D. (Ed) *Research Training for Social Scientists* London: Sage

Weller, P. (2000) Insiders or Outsiders? Religion(s), State(s) and Society: Propositions for Europe. University of Derby Inaugural Lecture. Derby: University of Derby

Weller, P. (2005) *Time for a Change* London: Continuum

Weller, P. and Purdam, K. (eds) (2000) *Religious Discrimination in England and Wales – Interim Report* Derby: Religious Resource and Research Centre, University of Derby

Wells, G. (1986) *The Meaning Makers: Children learning language and using language to learn.* Portsmouth, NH: Heinemann.

Wiggin, K.D. (1892) *Children's Rights: A Book of Nursery Logic* New York: Houghton Mifflin

Willis, J. and Ross, T. (1988) *Dr Xargles Book of Earthlets: an Alien's view of earth babies* London: Red Fox

Woodhead, M. and Faulkner, D. (2000) Subjects, Objects or Participants? In Christensen, P. and James, A. (Eds) (2000) *Research with Children, Perspectives and Practices* London: Falmer

Wright, C. (1998) 'Caught in the Crossfire': reflections of a black female ethnographer. In Connolly, P and Troyna, B. (Eds) (1998) *Researching Racism in Education – Politics, Theory and Practice.* Maidenhead: Open University Press

Wright, A. (2003) Freedom, Equality, Fraternity? Towards a Liberal Defence of Faith Community Schools pp 142-152 In *British Journal of Religious Education* Vol 25:2 Spring 2003

Wright, A. (2004) The justification of compulsory religious education: a response to Professor White *British Journal of Religious Education* Vol 26 no 2pp 165-174

Wright, P. (2002) Dark ages ban on Muslim scarf *Times Educational Supplement* 13 December

Index